fruit and vegetable growing in pictures

Ray Procter

Illustrated by Craig Warwick

Wolfe

First published 1976 by
Wolfe Publishing Ltd
10 Earlham Street
London WC2H 9LP

© Wolfe Publishing 1976

ISBN 0 7234 0695 2

Printed in Great Britain
by Ebenezer Baylis & Son Ltd
The Trinity Press, Worcester, and London

contents

A wide range of subjects is dealt with in picture-and-caption treatment in the Wolfe Pictorial Handbooks and the Wolfe Long Books.

THE WOLFE PICTORIAL HANDBOOKS

THE WOLFE LONG BOOKS

before you start

If you are new to the home growing of fruit and vegetables, this book is for you. I have tried to provide all the essential information for you to achieve success. You may think that some of the pictures are glimpses of the obvious but this is intentional. I, personally, have often found that a simple picture of a simple operation can be very reassuring, confirming that one has interpreted the author's instructions correctly. And pictures are sometimes easier to carry in your head than words. The metric equivalents given throughout this book are what might be called horticultural equivalents, rounded up or down, and near enough for gardening purposes. If you want more precise equivalents, some are given in the table below.

To grow as much fruit and vegetables in your garden as you can is sound sense. It is one way to beat inflation and if you increase your spendable income by saving on grocer's bills, remember there is no tax on this. And produce straight from your garden is so much tastier and fresher than anything you can buy. Good luck.

RAY PROCTER

METRIC EQUIVALENTS

1 in = 2.54 cm	1 cm = 0.394 in
1 ft = 30.48 cm	
1 yd = 0.914 m	1 m = 3.281 ft
1 sq yd = 0.836 sq m	1 sq m = 10.764 sq ft
1 pint = 0.568 litres	1 litre = 1.760 pints
1 gal = 4.546 litres	
1 oz = 28.35 g	1 g = 0.035 ozs
1 lb = 0.454 kg	1 kg = 2.205 lb

Fahrenheit to Celsius (Centigrade)

F	C	C	F
32	0.0	1	33.8
40	4.4	5	41.0
45	7.2	10	50.0
50	10.0	15	59.0
55	12.8	20	68.0
60	15.6	25	77.0
65	18.3	30	86.0
70	21.1		

groundwork
tools you will need

For growing both fruit and vegetables you must have certain tools. Others, although not essential, make work easier. Always buy the best you can afford: it is far better to have a few really good tools than many of inferior quality which may let you down just when you need them most.

1   For the initial preparation of the land you will need:
1. A garden line. 2. A spade. This should have a D-shaped handle, a shaft of a length to suit you and a medium-sized blade, of stainless steel if you can possibly afford it. 3. A digging fork. 4. A barrow, preferably with a thick rubber-tyred wheel.

2   For making seedbeds you will need an iron-toothed rake and a draw-hoe.

3   For later cultivation, a Dutch hoe and a pronged cultivator.

4   For planting you will need a metal-shod dibber, a small handfork and a trowel. Again, you will not regret the extra cost if the last two are of stainless steel.

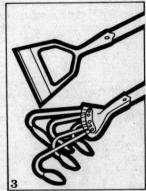

5   A measuring rod will be wanted but you can make your own with a straight piece of wood at least 2 metres long (about 6 ft 7 in). Make shallow saw-cuts to indicate centimetres and metres down one side and inches and feet on another.

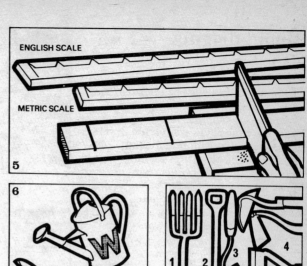

6   A watering can with detachable roses is essential. It is also advisable to have a second one reserved solely for weedkillers and conspicuously marked.

7   Other tools which will make work lighter are: 1. A fork with flat prongs for digging potatoes. 2. A shovel for moving soil, sand etc. 3. A hand hoe for onion beds etc. 4. Various hoes of differing shapes.

8   For fruit growing you must have pruning tools. Secateurs are safer than a knife and these can be either: The anvil type (1), the scimitar type (2) or the parrot beak type (3) provided the latter are really sharp. For cutting larger branches a pruning saw (4) which cuts on the 'pull' (instead of the 'push') is easier than an ordinary saw. A bow saw (5) will cut the biggest branches.

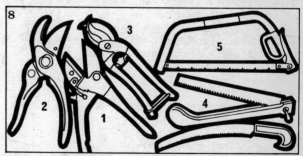

9   A sprayer will be necessary for fruit and vegetables. It pays to buy the best you can afford with a long lance.

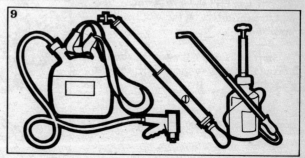

single digging

Before either fruit or vegetables are grown the ground must be prepared. This involves digging to eliminate perennial weed roots, to improve surface drainage, to improve the physical structure of the soil and enrich it with manure and decaying vegetable matter where necessary. The beginner may have heard of 'no-digging' theories but would be well advised to follow orthodox practice until he has disposed of all perennial weeds and he himself has gained in knowledge and experience.

1   With a new plot start by cutting down all top hamper. Burn woody material.

2   Cut through the surface of the turf in strips, to a depth of about 5 cm (2 in).

3   Cut through the roots of the grass with the spade and prise up.

4   Stack the old turf to rot, dusting the layers alternately with hydrated lime and sulphate of ammonia, or with proprietary compost-maker.

5   Now divide the plot to be dug into two halves, lengthways.

6   The soil from the first trench excavated will fill the last. Arrow indicates the direction the work will proceed.

7   Start by taking out a trench about 30 cm (1 ft) wide to the full depth of the spade blade.

8   Take the excavated soil to a point close to where digging will finish.

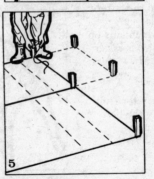

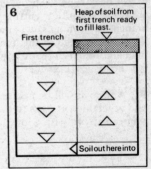

First trench

Heap of soil from first trench ready to fill last.

Soil out here into

9 Spread evenly over the surface of the still undug land any manure or compost to be worked in.

10 Transfer a portion of this manure or compost to the bottom of the trench.

11 Now, standing on the undug side, insert the spade about 15 cm (6 in) from the edge of the trench and at one end.

12 If the spade is pressed in at an angle the soil will not be cultivated so deeply.

13 Press the spade to its fullest depth, your weight on your foot on the tread.

14 Now by pressing down the handle, lever up the spadeful of soil.

15 Slide the other hand down the spade shaft and lift. Twist the spade over as you throw the soil forward, thus inverting it, to fill the trench in front.

16 To avoid backache, take it easily at first and try to keep the back concave as you work and lift with the legs and arms rather than with the back.

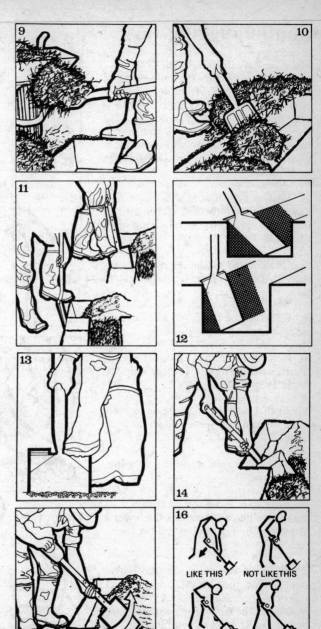

double digging

So far we have described only the simplest form of digging — single digging. Where drainage is poor and deep-rooting crops are to be grown it is advisable to break up the lower soil and double digging (also known as mock trenching) is resorted to. Some successful vegetable growers double dig one third of their area each winter.

1 Mark out the plot as with single digging but make the first trench 50 cm (or 2 ft) wide and to the full depth of the spade's blade.

2 Clean out all the loose crumbs of soil until the bottom of the trench is neat and tidy.

3 Wheel all the excavated soil to a spot alongside where you will finish.

4 Now break up the bottom of the trench with the digging fork, working to the full depth of the tines.

5 At this stage any manure or compost to be worked in is spread down the trench.

6 Mix the manure with the soil, using the fork.

7 Now mark out a second trench with the garden line and turn the soil, inverting it spadeful by spadeful, to fill the first trench.

8 The work now proceeds trench by trench across the plot. This diagram makes the operation clear: A. The first trench. B. The first trench with bottom broken up. C. First trench filled by second. D. Second trench with bottom broken up.

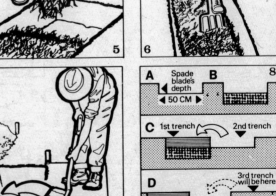

A Spade blade's depth
◄ 50 CM ►
B
8

C 1st trench   2nd trench

D 3rd trench will be here

breaking grassland

1 Where grassland is to be broken up the turf can be dug in to rot in situ. Pare the turf from the first 50 cm (or 2 ft) wide strip, stacking roughly near where you will finish.

2 Dig out the soil to a spade blade's depth from the first trench and transfer to near the heap of turf ready for filling in the final trench.

3 Clean the crumbs from the trench and break up the bottom with the digging fork.

4 Pare off the turf from the second 50 cm (or 2 ft) wide strip, throwing it upside down in the first trench.

5 Chop the turf up with the spade.

6 Dig the top soil from the second strip, throwing it, inverted, on the chopped turf.

ridging

Winter frost tends to pulverise soil. To expose the maximum surface to this action (particularly beneficial for heavy soil) adopt the form of single digging called ridging. Divide the plot into strips 1 metre (or 1 yd) wide. Now make the usual single digging trenches across each strip in turn, throwing the soil from the outer sides of each short trench towards the centre as you invert it. Thus ridges will be formed down the middle of the strip. Break down the ridges in spring.

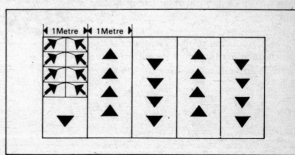

draining wet land

Drainage is important because wet land discourages helpful micro-organisms which aid growth. Good drainage is vital for fruit trees and bushes which can be, literally, drowned in winter. Digging and the working in of rotting vegetable matter will improve surface drainage.

1   Heavy soils are more likely to be ill-drained and sometimes trouble is caused by a hard pan or layer about 30 cm (1 ft) down formed by repeated ploughing in years gone by. Double digging should break up this pan.

2   Where there is a ditch into which water may be discharged, poorly drained ground can be drastically improved by laying down a herringbone pattern of earthenware agricultural land drainpipes.

3   Dig the trenches for the drainpipes first and test with a spirit level to see they always slope towards the outlet.

4   Depth depends on the soil — 45 cm (18 in) in clay, 60 cm (24 in) in medium loam, at the shallowest point, sloping at about 1 in 50 to 100.

5   Lay the drainpipes on a bed of rubble with 1¼ cm (½ in) gaps between and cover with pieces of slate, broken tile or coarse rubble.

6   Spread coarse rubble, stones or brickbats along the drain to within 30 cm (1 ft) of the surface and return the top soil.

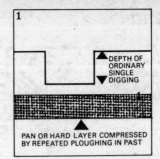

1 — DEPTH OF ORDINARY SINGLE DIGGING / PAN OR HARD LAYER COMPRESSED BY REPEATED PLOUGHING IN PAST

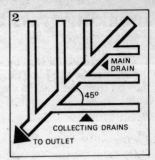

2 — MAIN DRAIN / 45° / COLLECTING DRAINS / TO OUTLET

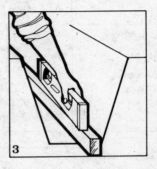

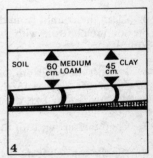

4 — SOIL / 60 cm MEDIUM LOAM / 45 cm CLAY

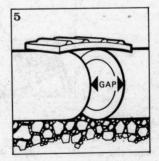

3

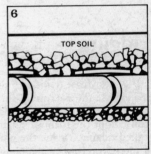

5 — GAP

6 — TOP SOIL

7   The side drains of the herringbone system should join the main drain at an angle of 45 degrees, pointing towards the outlet.

8   Don't attempt to make close joints. Cover these main junctions with whole slates or tiles.

9   Side drains should join the main drain on alternate sides and never opposite each other.

10   To avoid frost damage, use glazed piping for the end of the drain disgorging into the ditch.

11   Block the last pipe with wire netting to prevent the entry of debris and vermin.

12   Where no ditch is available, make a soakaway. Dig a deep hole and fill with brickbats and coarse rubble.

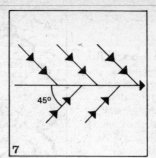

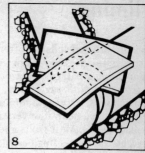

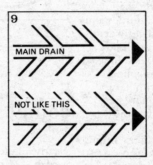

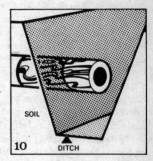

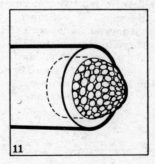

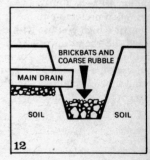

liming

Badly drained soils are often too acid for successful growing. A few vegetables, including asparagus, beetroot, cabbage, carrots, cauliflower, celery, Jerusalem artichokes, lettuce, onions and parsley, do best in a neutral or very slightly alkaline soil. Most fruits and a few vegetables, including beans, broccoli (winter cauliflower), Brussels sprouts, cucumbers, endive, kale, leeks, parsnips, peas, potatoes, radish, rhubarb, shallots and garlic, spinach, tomatoes, turnips and vegetable marrows, prefer a slightly acid soil. Excess acidity can be neutralised chemically by sprinkling hydrated lime over the bare surface. Never mix lime with any fertiliser or apply with natural manure. Ground in which manure has been dug in should be limed (on the surface) several weeks later.

To test soil for acidity you can use litmus paper (A) or pour a little dilute hydrochloric acid on a soil sample (B) — if it fizzes, it does not need lime — but these are very approximate indicators. It is much preferable to buy a soil testing outfit which you use with distilled water and the chemicals provided, the resultant colour reaction being compared with those on a chart supplied with the set (C) and lime, if required, then being applied according to directions.

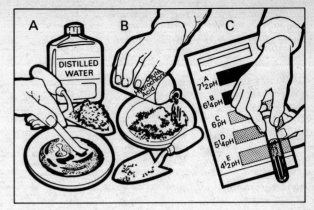

compost making

Nearly all the vegetable waste of the garden — leaves, mowings, finished plants — can be recycled via the compost heap. Well-made compost can be the equal of, if not superior to, farmyard manure in plant nutrients and soil-improving organic matter. The only waste matter which should be burnt are plants which are diseased or bearing seeds and woody stems and prunings. There are many methods of compost-making: here is one.

1 Since air is essential for decomposition the compost heap must not be too wide or too high. It can be any length. If the site is well-drained, excavate the site to a depth of a spade's blade and 90cm (1 yd) wide.

2 For the sake of neatness you can surround the compost heap on three sides with wire netting or plastic mesh netting. The height should not exceed 90 cm (1 yd).

3 Put down a 15 cm (6 in) layer of vegetable waste, mixing the material well together.

4 Chop into short pieces any soft stems as you proceed. Water if dry and tread.

5 Now put on a layer 1 to 2½ cm (½ to 1 in) thick of stable or farmyard manure, or, if not available, sprinkle sulphate of ammonia, a handful per sq m (sq yd).

6 Cover the manure from view with another but thinner layer of vegetable matter and sprinkle with hydrated lime at 225 g per sq m (¾ oz per sq ft).

7 Then put on a layer of soil 1 to 2½ cm (½ to 1 in) thick. Follow with another thick (15 cm or 6 in) layer of vegetable matter continuing this until the heap is 90 cm (3 ft) high and a layer of soil completes.

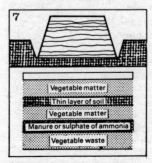

8 Water in dry weather and after 4 weeks in summer or 6 to 8 weeks in autumn or winter turn the heap, bringing the outside to the centre. For this purpose it is convenient to have a second site alongside. Instead of sulphate of ammonia a proprietary accelerator may be used according to the maker's directions.

Vegetable matter
Thin layer of soil
Vegetable matter
Manure or sulphate of ammonia
Vegetable waste

preparing for fruit planting

Having decided to grow fruit, it is not enough just to order some trees and bushes: you should start to prepare the soil in July or August ready for autumn planting. Good drainage is essential and deep digging will help to ensure this. With average good garden soil previously cultivated it is seldom necessary to add manure in advance of planting tree fruits. Light, sandy, gravelly or chalky soils need to have plenty of manure or compost worked into the subsoil. Soft fruits need relatively more food in their early stages and manure or compost should almost always be incorporated, really liberally in the lighter soils. A high organic soil content is also necessary for soft fruits to ensure adequate moisture throughout summer.

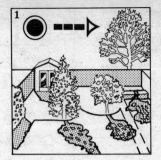

thinking ahead

1   In deciding where you will plant fruit think of where the sun rises and sets and what shade will be cast by buildings, trees and fences.

2   Don't plant fruit close to trees or hedges which will always try to take the lion's share of any manure you provide.

3   Walls provide warmth and shelter for trained trees and make protection from birds easy.

4   But remember the foot of a wall is the driest place in the garden and plenty of moisture-holding compost or peat should be incorporated.

5 Be wary of the space between adjoining houses which can act as a funnel concentrating a cold east wind on vulnerable spring blossom.

6 If possible group trees together as this makes spraying and other cultural attention easier.

7 Soft fruit grown in a block together is easier and cheaper to protect from birds. (See also page 74 .)

8 Prepare an emergency temporary planting place for new fruits in a sheltered spot. Cover with a sheet of plastic to keep it dry.

9 Cover the emergency temporary planting site (heeling in, this is called) with straw, dry leaves, bracken or peat to prevent it freezing.

10 Finally cover the protective litter with another sheet of plastic to keep it dry.

11 To prevent the 'eiderdown' blowing away, weight it down with bricks or put a little soil all round the edge.

12 Again, thinking ahead, a good supply of topsoil heaped in a dry place or well covered from rain may well enable planting even when soil conditions are otherwise unpropitious.

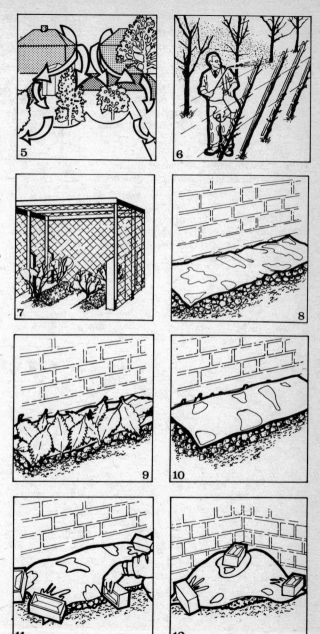

13   A supply of peat should be in readiness. This must be slightly moist for use. Either pour water into the plastic bag . . .

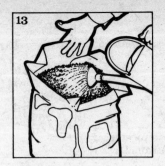

14   . . . or put the peat into some container and add water. It will take hours, even days, for the dry peat as purchased to take up sufficient moisture.

15   Actual planting places may be protected with litter and plastic to keep dry. This will enable planting to proceed in frosty weather.

16   But never take out planting holes a day or more in advance of planting. If it rains, such holes merely become sumps collecting surface water.

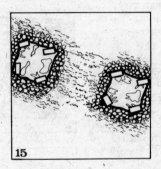

stakes and supports

All fruit trees need support when first planted. Trained trees and those on dwarfing rootstocks will need support all their lives. Stakes and other supports should be prepared in advance of planting. The length of the stakes and the number required will depend on the type of tree concerned and the system of staking adopted.

1 Peeled chestnut stakes are best, 5 to 7.6 cm (2 to 3 in) in diameter. The part to be buried and for some 15 cm (6 in) above should be treated with preservative.

2 If you have to treat the ends yourself, select a copper-based preservative and leave the ends to soak for a week. Painting with a brush does not achieve sufficient penetration.

3 A saturated solution of copper sulphate (bluestone) is a cheap preservative but a metallic container must never be used. Soak for ten days.

4 Trees may be supported by single or double vertical stakes or a single oblique stake pointing towards the prevailing wind.

5 It is sound sense to provide a 3 m (10 ft) vertical stake for dwarf bush-type trees, 45 cm to 61 cm (18 in − 2 ft) being buried. Later, heavily-laden branches can be suspended from this, maypole fashion.

6 For espalier and fan-trained trees provide horizontal wires (2.5 mm, gauge 12, galvanised) at 30 cm (1 ft) intervals.

7 Use an adjustable straining bolt at the end of each wire to keep it taut.

8 For cordons provide three wires strained between stout posts at about 3 m (10 ft) intervals.

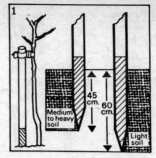

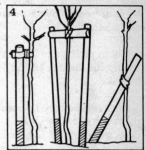

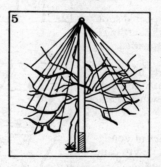

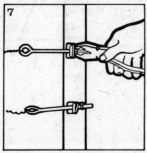

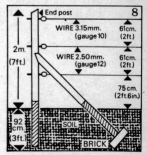

fastening fruit trees

Besides having stakes or other supports ready in advance you must have the means of fastening the tree. It is not good enough to hunt round the house for an odd length of string when your new trees arrive.

1   Plastic ties are good because they are easily adjustable and neither rot nor harbour pests. They are available in various sizes.

2   With plastic ties buffers are provided to prevent the tree from chafing against its stake.

3   Stout cord may be used for tying. Pad the tree itself with sacking, cloth or old inner tube and lap the cord between tree and stake to make a buffer.

4   Fastenings should be inspected soon after planting in case, with the settling of soil, the tree has become suspended.

5   Check fastenings regularly because with growth they soon become too tight. Constrictions can check growth and allow canker disease an entry.

6   Cordons and the branches of young fans and espaliers should be tied to canes (which have been fastened to the supporting wires). Use soft string for this.

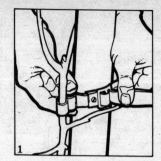
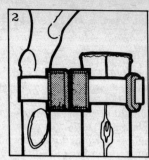

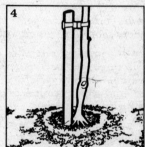

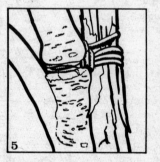
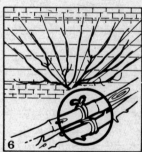

marking
out the fruit plot

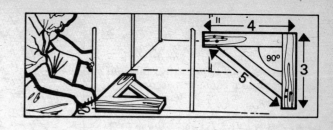

Before fruit planting begins decide
exactly where each tree or bush is to go
and mark the spot with a stick.

When marking out a plot for planting
make sure the corners are true right
angles. Remember that some right-angled
triangles have sides in the ratio of 3, 4
and 5, the longest side being opposite the
right angle.

when the
fruit trees arrive

If you buy your fruit trees, bushes or
canes from a distance, they may arrive at
an inopportune moment, the roots may
have dried out and they may have been
damaged slightly in lifting or transit.

1   Immediately the new trees arrive
open the package so that air can get to
them.

2   If you cannot plant at once, protect
from frost and never stand the trees
where a wind can play on the roots.

3   An outhouse or garage is a suitable
temporary shelter but beware of mice
which may gnaw the roots.

4   Before planting examine the roots
closely and shorten to sound growth any
which have been damaged, making
sloping cuts on the underside.

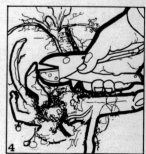

5   If the roots have dried out, soak in water for an hour.

6   Where planting has to be delayed, 'heel in' outdoors temporarily. Take out a trench just deep enough to accommodate the roots.

7   Lay the fruit trees along the sloping side of this trench.

8   Then fill it with soil up to the nursery soil marks on the stems and tread firm with the heel.

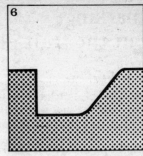

tree fruit planting distances

Where two figures are given the wider spacing should be allowed on rich soil or when the variety in question is known to be particularly vigorous or on a strong-growing rootstock. The smaller figure should be regarded as the minimum distance to allow on average soil. It is always better to allow a little too much space rather than not enough. Where no figures are given for the distance between rows it is because in such instances the trees are usually trained against walls.

Kind of fruit	Form of tree	Distance between trees in row		Distance between rows	
		metres	feet	metres	feet
APPLE	Standard or half-standard	7.3—9.0	24—30	7.3—9.0	24—30
	Bush	3.6—5.5	12—18	3.6—5.5	12—18
	Dwarf Bush	2.5—3.0	8—10	2.5—3.0	8—10
	Pyramid	1.0—1.2	3½— 4	2.1	7
	Single cordon	0.75—0.9	2½— 3	1.8	6
	Fan	3.0—4.5	10—15	3.0—4.5	10—15
	Espalier	3.0—4.5	10—15	3.0—4.5	10—15
	Spindlebush	1.8—2.6	6— 8½	3.6—4.3	12—14
APRICOT	Fan	4.5—5.5	15—18	—	—
CHERRY, Acid	Bush	4.5—5.5	15—18	4.5—5.5	15—18
	Fan	3.0—5.5	10—18	4.5	15
CHERRY, Sweet	Standard	9.1—12.2	30—40	9.1—12.2	30—40
	Bush	7.6—10.7	25—35	7.6—10.7	25—35
	Fan	5.5—7.3	18—24	—	—
FIG	Bush	4.5—6.0	15—20	4.5—6.0	15—20
	Fan	2.5—6.0	8—20	—	—
NECTARINE	Fan	3.5—5.5	12—18	—	—
NUT	Bush	3.5	12	3.5	12
PEACH	Bush	5.5	18	5.5	18
	Fan	3.5—5.5	12—18	—	—
PEAR	Standard or half-standard	7.3—11.0	24—36	7.3—11.0	24—36
	Bush	3.5—4.5	12—15	3.5—4.5	12—15
	Dwarf bush	3.0—4.3	10—14	3.0—4.3	10—14
	Pyramid	1.0	3½	2.1	7
	Single cordon	0.6—0.9	2—3	1.8	6
	Fan	3.5—6.0	12—20	2.5—3.0	8—10
	Espalier	3.5—6.0	12—20	2.5—3.0	8—10
PLUM, GAGE & DAMSON	Standard or half-standard	4.5—7.6	15—25	4.5—7.6	15—25
	Bush	3.5—4.5	12—15	3.5—4.5	12—15
	Pyramid	3.0—3.5	10—12	3.0—3.5	10—12
	Fan	3.5—5.5	12—18	2.5—3.0	8—10
QUINCE	Half-standard	5.5—7.3	18—24	5.5—7.3	18—24
	Bush	3.5—5.5	12—18	3.5—5.5	12—18

soft fruit planting distances

These figures should be regarded as the
minimum distances to allow on average
soil. On very rich soil allow slightly more.

Kind of fruit		Distance between plants in row		Distance between rows	
		metres	feet	metres	feet
BLACKBERRY	Merton Thornless and Denver Thornless	1.8	6	2.1	7
	Most varieties	3.0	10	2.1	7
	Himalaya Giant	3.6—6.0	12—20	2.1	7
BLACK CURRANT		1.8	6	1.8	6
BLUEBERRY		1.8	6	1.8	6
GOOSEBERRY	Bush	1.5	5	1.5	5
	Single cordon	0.4	1¼	1.5	5
	Double-U cordons	0.9	3	1.5	5
LOGANBERRY and other hybrids		2.5—3.6	8—12	1.8	6
RASPBERRY		0.45	1½	1.8	6
RED & WHITE CURRANT	Bush	1.5	5	1.5	5
	Single cordon	0.4	1¼	1.5	5
	Double-U cordons	0.9	3	1.5	5
STRAWBERRY	Most varieties	0.45	1½	0.75	2½
	Elista	0.23	¾	0.75	2½
	Alpine	0.3	1	0.3	1

planting fruit

The planting season for fruit trees, bushes and canes extends from October or November until March, the period of dormancy. Sometimes fruits, more often the soft fruits, can be purchased growing in containers and these may be transplanted at other times provided the roots are not disturbed. Nevertheless, autumn planting is always preferable, the earlier the better provided the soil is moist and friable, never wet and sticky.

how to plant

1   The first step in planting is to take out a hole wide and deep enough for all the roots to be fully spread out in their natural growing position.

2   Break up the soil in the bottom of the hole, using a digging fork.

3   Draw a little soil from the edges of the hole towards the centre to make a shallow mound on which the tree can 'sit'.

4   Lay a straight plank or plant stake across the hole to indicate soil level.

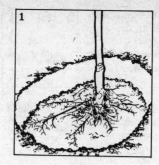

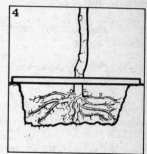

5   Check the tree's depth. The soil mark on the stem indicates its depth in the nursery which is probably correct. In grafted trees the union between rootstock and top must be at least 10 cm (4 in) above soil level.

6   Stakes should be driven in before covering the roots so that the latter are not damaged. From this stage on an assistant will be a great advantage.

7   Scatter a few handfuls of moist peat directly over the roots . . .

8   . . . and then start returning topsoil with the spade.

9   Don't be afraid to use your fingers to work soil intimately around the roots.

10   Make firm after each few spadefuls of soil. Firm planting is essential.

11   If the soil is on the poor side sprinkle a double handful of sterilised bonemeal over the soil being returned.

12   Or, instead of bonemeal, topdress with a general garden fertiliser according to the maker's directions and rake into the surface.

13 To preserve soil moisture mulch 5 cm (2 in) deep with rotted compost or well-rotted manure a little farther than the roots extend, keeping this well clear of the stem.

14 Finally trees should be fastened securely but temporarily to their stakes.

15 In rural areas where rabbits or hares may cause irrevocable injury protect the stem of the young tree with a plastic or wire-netting tree guard.

16 Plant cordon trees at an angle of 45° pointing towards the north. At the union the rootstock should be underneath.

17 When planting a tree against a wall (a very dry spot), set it 15 to 23 cm (6 to 9 in) away and incline backwards to the wall.

18 Where poor drainage cannot be remedied, fork the planting place and make quite a shallow hole.

19 Stand the tree in position, almost on the surface and provide a very strong stake.

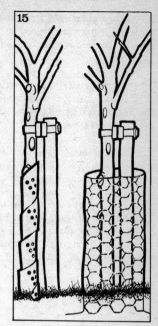

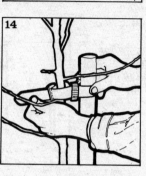

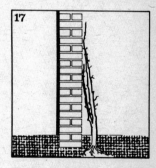

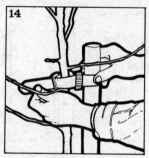

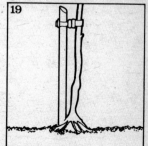

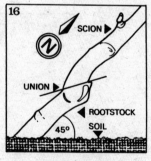

20   Draw in top soil from the vicinity until the roots are covered to the normal depth. The tree is thus virtually set upon a mound.

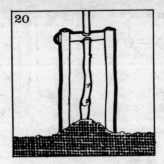

21   Where several trees are to be planted their exact positioning is facilitated by the use of a planting board. Prepare a plank about 1.8 m (6 ft) long as here.

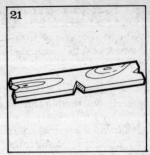

22   Set the board against the cane marking the spot where the tree is to be and insert a cane in each end notch.

23   Remove the board and the middle cane and make the planting hole. The tree is then roughly positioned and the board replaced. The stem of the tree should coincide with the middle notch.

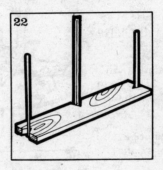

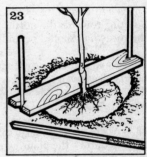

how to grow tree fruit

Fruit trees are often purchased already trained by the nurseryman to conform to one of several recognised patterns, shown below. It should be borne in mind that the silhouette of a round tree (frames 1, 2 and 3) will look much the same from any angle, that of a flat-trained tree (frames 4 and 5) will not.

shapes of trees

1   Standards and half-standards are trees on tall trunks or legs. They are too large for normal gardens. A standard apple or pear tree (left) has a leg of about 2 m (6½ ft) and a half-standard about 1.4 m (4½ ft).

2   Bush trees normally have a leg of about 0.75 m (2½ ft) but apples and pears can be grown as dwarf bushes with a leg of only about 0.45 m (1½ ft).

3   In a pyramid the branches radiate from the central stem, gradually decreasing in length.

4   Cordons are basically trees without branches. Apples and pears are often grown as oblique cordons (left). Red and white currants and gooseberries are often grown as single upright cordons but may also be trained as single-U cordons or double-U cordons.

5   The best fans are as seen on the left, but nowadays many nursery-grown fans are as at the centre, a form grown more quickly and hence more cheaply. Espaliers, on the right, may be of many tiers but one, two or three are most common.

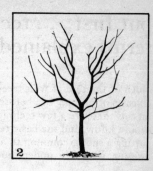
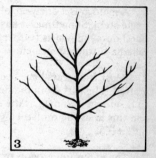
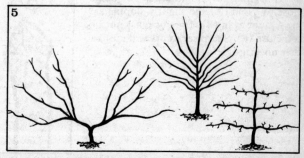
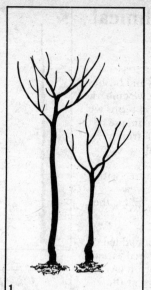
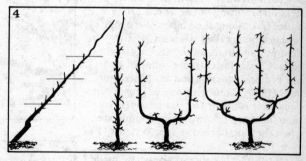

but first . . . technical terms explained

Much of the care of fruit trees and bushes consists of pruning but before we embark on this there are a few technical terms we should know, and the basic technique of cutting a shoot, common to all fruit pruning, should be understood.

1   A maiden is a one-year-old tree with a single stem. Sometimes it has a few sideshoots, known as feathers, and is then called a feathered maiden.

2   Most fruit trees have been budded or grafted. The part from the desired variety to be grown is known as the scion (A) and this joins the rootstock (B) at the union (C).

3   The extension growth of a branch or stem made during one season is called a leader (A). Along the branch there may be sideshoots, called laterals (B). The thin, pointed buds on shoots are growth buds (C), the fatter, more rounded buds will produce blossom and are called fruit buds (D). A shoot with one or more fruit buds on it is a spur (E) and in course of time these can become quite complicated when they are known as spur systems (F).

4   A pruning cut should always be made close to a bud (A) and slightly sloping as in (A), not as in (B). The cut must not be too close (C). Sharp secateurs will ensure that no snag is left (D).

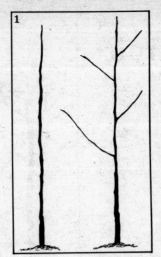

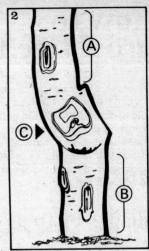

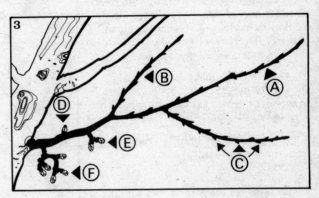

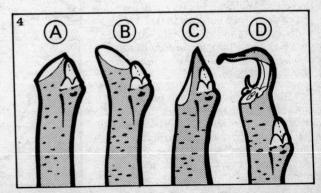

apples and pears as bush trees

The pruning of a fruit tree in its early years is directed towards shaping it to the desired form. Usually trees are purchased at a stage when this shaping has been begun, if not completed, but to plant a maiden and do all the shaping yourself is very interesting and also saves your pocket. Normally a new tree should be pruned at once according to its age.

1   To form a bush tree, the first step is to cut a maiden to a bud about 0.5 to 0.6 m (20 to 24 in) above the ground.

2   Select a point where there are three or four buds evenly spaced round the stem.

3   Unwanted, badly-placed buds may be rubbed off with the thumb.

4   In the first summer these selected top few buds will produce shoots to form the first main branches.

5   In the second winter cut back the best shoots (up to four) to form branches to a third to half their length, pruning to outward-pointing buds to keep the centre open.

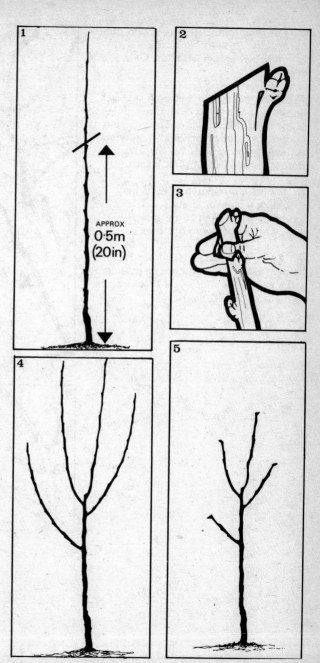

APPROX
0·5m
(20in)

6 Cut back shoots from the main stem not required as branches to the fourth bud in winter and pinch at the sixth leaf in summer.

7 In the second summer each cut-back branch will now make several new shoots. In the third winter select about six to ten of these to make branches and prune to outward-pointing buds, cutting away from a third to half of their length.

8 Shoots not required as branches should be treated as laterals. Leave unpruned if less than 15 m (6 in), otherwise cut to the fourth bud.

9 A year later the pruned lateral should have developed one or more fruit buds and a new shoot which you now cut back to the first (growth) bud.

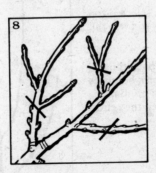

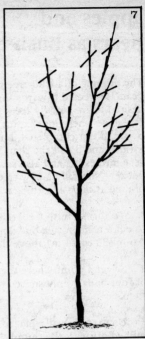

10　In the fourth winter, and from then on, the branch leaders should be cut back less drastically, according to vigour of growth. Cut back a third of the new growth if vigorous, up to two-thirds if weak. Winter cutting stimulates growth.

11　For four-year and older trees winter pruning also gives an opportunity to remove dead, diseased or damaged branches and misplaced ones which rub against one another.

12　With older trees, too, it may be necessary to remove branches to let in light to others.

13　Spur systems may also have become congested so that fruits themselves are crowded. Overlong spur systems should be shortened and some may be removed entirely.

14　Some apple varieties and a few pears are tip-bearers. These tend to form fruit buds at the tip of one-year-old shoots. If the laterals on such trees were treated in the way described above most of the potential blossom would be cut out year after year.

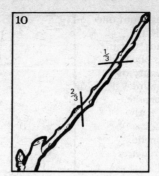

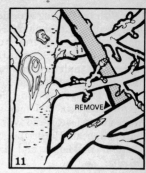

Under-cut to avoid tearing

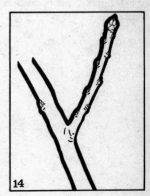

15   With tip-bearing varieties about one third of all shoots should be left unpruned to develop fruit buds. Cut the other two-thirds of laterals to one bud. Tip-bearing apples include Beauty of Bath, Bramley's Seedling, Edward VII, Ellison's Orange, Laxton's Fortune, Laxton's Superb, Tydeman's Early Worcester, Winston and Worcester Pearmain; pears Hessle, Jargonelle, Josephine de Malines and Marguerite Marrillat.

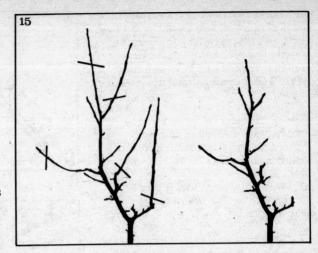

16   Bush pear trees on quince rootstocks are formed in the same way as apples but with slightly less severe pruning in the early years. Tip-bearing varieties, having a more weeping habit, should have a leg of at least 75 cm (30 in). Established pears need pruning rather harder than apples.

17   When bush trees are established and if growing well — and only if — they will benefit from the summer pruning of laterals only. When the bases of the new shoots become woody, from early August until September, cut back to about 13 cm (5 in). Spread this operation over several weeks.

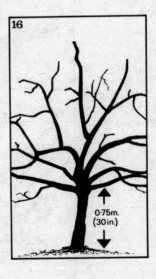

0·75m.
(30 in.)

18 Some varieties tend to crop heavily one year and barely, if at all, the next. To counteract this habit thin the blossom buds in the year when a heavy crop is expected. Rub the blossom buds off before they open, leaving only one per spur.

19 The thinning of fruit after it has set will also help to reduce biennial bearing and will improve fruit size and quality. Do this before the natural drop of fruitlets occurs in June and July. Use sharp, pointed scissors and remove the 'king' apples first — the central one in each cluster. Reduce to one fruit per spur.

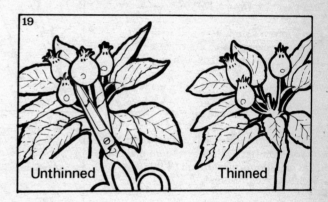

Unthinned   Thinned

apples and pears as cordons

A popular space-saving way of growing apples and pears is as oblique cordons, in single file against wire supports arranged as on page 21 (frame 8). Start by buying 2- or 3-year cordons or order maidens specifying M 9 rootstock (for good soil), M 26 or MM 106 (for poorer soil) for apples and quince C rootstock, when available, (for good soil) or quince A (for poorer soil) for pears. Plant as described on page 29 (frame 16).

1   Cordons should be tied with soft string to canes which are themselves tied securely to the horizontal wires.

2   The lowest tie should be made near the union. Always leave space for growth and inspect ties regularly.

3   No initial pruning is usually necessary but if you start with a feathered maiden, cut sideshoots over 10 cm (4 in) long back to the third bud.

4   In the case of tip-bearing varieties (see page 36, frame 15) it is advisable to cut a maiden back by one quarter.

5   Future pruning is done in summer and starts when the laterals are mature, for apples about mid-July in southern England, later in the north, a week or so earlier for pears.

6   When laterals reach this stage, cut each back to the third leaf beyond the basal cluster. Deal with previously immature sideshoots in mid-September.

7   Repeat this procedure annually. Cut any shoots arising from previously pruned laterals to one leaf beyond the basal cluster.

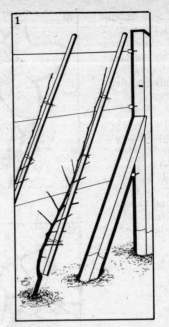

1

2

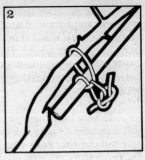

3

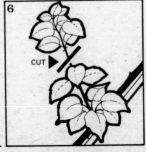

4

CUT HERE   ¼

5

DARK GREEN LEAVES

23cm. 9in. OR MORE

BECOMING WOODY

MAIN STEM

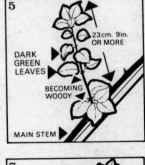

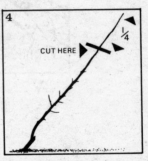

6

CUT

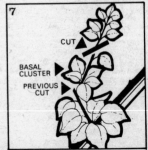

7

CUT

BASAL CLUSTER

PREVIOUS CUT

8 If the shoots pruned in midsummer send out further growth, cut these new shoots back to one bud in early October.

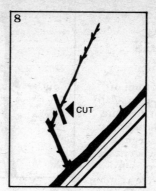

9 When the leader passes the top wire, give it more space by unfastening the cane from the wires and lowering by at least 5 degrees. Then re-tie.

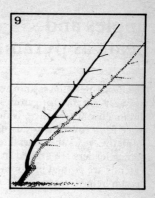

10 This lowering can often be done three times, but by then leader growth has usually ceased. If it has not, cut back as necessary in May.

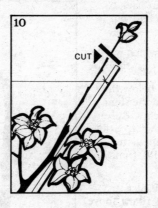

11 The triangle of unoccupied space above the first cordon in the row should be filled by two vertical laterals, subsequently pruning each as a cordon.

12 To encourage laterals to grow where desired (as in previous picture) and to furnish otherwise bare lengths of stem, resort to notching in May, cutting a tiny half-moon of bark away immediately above the bud to be stimulated into growth.

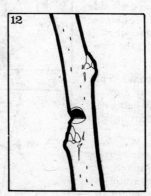

13 Normally cordon leaders do not need pruning until they reach their height limit. Exceptions are tip-bearing varieties and others which are growing poorly: then cut the leader back by a third of its length in winter.

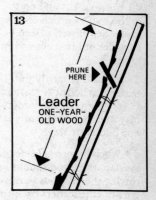

apples and pears as pyramids

The dwarf pyramid is another form of tree very suitable for gardens, particularly the smallest where there is not even the space for a row of cordons. During the formative years the central leader and branch leaders are pruned in winter. Laterals are pruned in summer, each branch being treated as if it were a cordon.

1 Starting with a maiden, cut back to about 50 cm (20 in). The top bud will produce a vertical shoot.

2 Rub out the second bud which would also produce a competing vertical shoot.

3 Select three or four buds below the top two, evenly spaced round the stem, to form the first tier of branches. Rub out misplaced buds and notch above the two lowest chosen buds to stimulate them into growth (see page 39, frame 12).

4 The next winter cut the leader to a bud about 20 to 25 cm (8 to 10 in) above the previous cut and on the opposite side to the bud to which last year's cut was made. Select well placed buds for the next tier of branches and notch the two lowest.

5 Repeat annually until a convenient maximum height is reached, say 2 m (7 ft). Then cut the leaders by half in May and in subsequent years cut back to one bud each May.

6 When branches of neighbouring trees overlap, these too should be limited, cutting the previous year's extension growth (the leader) back to one bud at blossom time.

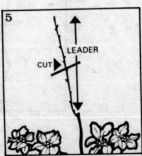

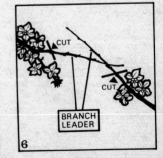

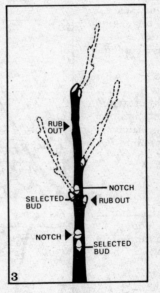

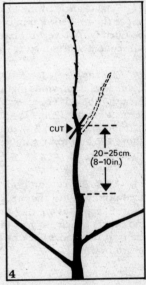

apples and pears as espaliers

The espalier or horizontally-trained tree is a useful shape for planting alongside borders or as a dividing screen between one part of the garden and another. Apples and pears are most amenable to this form of training. You can buy ready-formed espaliers with one, two or three tiers of branches but it is more interesting and much cheaper to grow your own, starting with a maiden.

1 Cut the maiden down to a bud having two buds beneath it, one on either side, between 30 and 45 cm (12-18 in) high. Notch above the lowest bud (see page 39, frame 12).

2 If any other buds, in addition to the selected three, start to grow, rub them out with the thumb.

3 As the three shoots develop tie the centre one to a vertical cane and the others to canes at about 45 degrees, using soft string.

4 If one shoot grows more quickly than the other, lower it slightly to check it.

5 At summer's end lower the two oblique canes and fasten to the lowest horizontal wire about 2.5 − 5 cm (1 − 2 in) above the origin of the two sideshoots.

6 Repeat this procedure annually for each tier of branches but when the top tier is reached permit only two buds to grow. Prune the laterals on the branches in summer, like cordons.

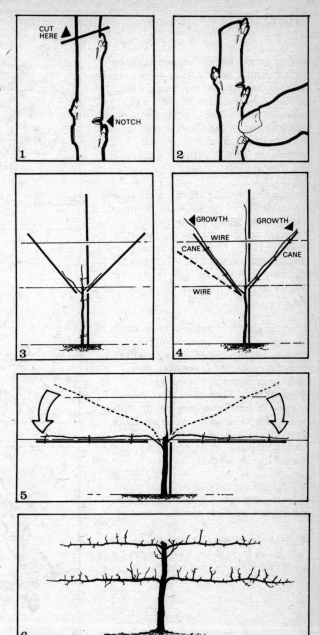

cherries

Sweet cherries are not very suitable for garden culture because they tend to make very big trees and at least two, of very carefully chosen varieties, have to be grown to provide for cross-pollination. Acid cherries of the Morello type are much easier because they are self-pollinating (so you need grow only one) and they are less vigorous.

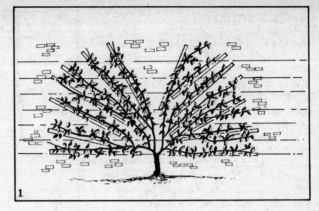

1   Morello cherries are often grown as fan-trained trees against walls. Although less vigorous than the sweet varieties, they still ought to be given a spread of 3 to 5.5 m (10 – 18 ft). The training of the fan is as shown on p. 48. Acid cherries may also be grown as bush trees and are pruned in their formative years like plums.

2   Acid cherries fruit mostly on wood of the previous year's growth and so pruning consists of cutting out older growth to encourage new. With younger, but established, trees cut into 2-year-old wood, as here. With older trees the pruning of some branches must be more drastic. Prune in spring when the buds have broken and growth buds can be easily identified. Fan-trained trees may be pruned like peaches.

3   To prevent disease infection paint over pruning cuts with a bitumastic tree paint made specially for the purpose.

4   When ripening all cherries need protection from birds. This is more easily given to wall trees than bushes.

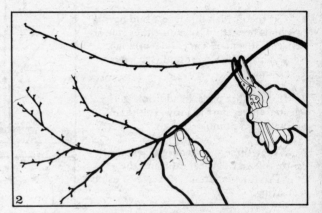

figs

Figs like warmth and sun and therefore do best in the south and west of Britain, especially if 'within sight of the sea'. They try to produce two crops in a year but we can only expect one to ripen outdoors in our climate. A light, shallow soil over chalk grows good figs: too rich a soil produces rampant growth at the expense of fruit.

1 Figs do best fan-trained against a southerly-facing wall. To prevent over-lush growth, restrict the roots by planting in an underground box, 90 cm (3 ft) deep with a 30 cm (1 ft) layer of brickbats or chalk lumps packed in the bottom.

2 No pruning is necessary the first year. Training a fan follows much the same lines as a peach (see page 44), spacing the branches out 30 cm (1 ft) apart and tying them in. Later, as cropping is at the end of ever-extending branches, a few branches should be cut back to short stubs each year in March to produce young replacements. Before the end of June stop all sideshoots at the fifth leaf and tie in a month later.

3 When pruning in spring cut out all dead wood. Cut back into healthy tissue (A) showing no stain at the centre. B depicts severe die-back infection and C slight infection.

4 Figs crop on the tips of shoots made the previous summer. In August a fruiting shoot will bear ripening fruits (A), second-crop fruits (B) which can never ripen and should be picked off, and embryo fruits (C) for next year's crop.

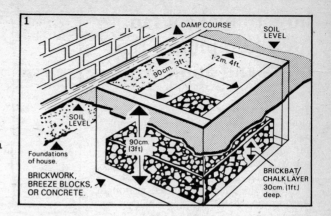

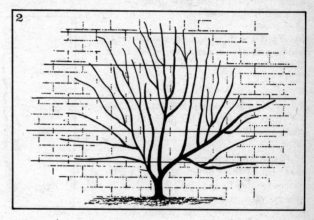

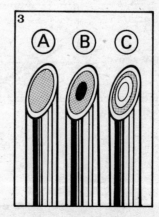

how to make a fan (peaches, plums, figs, pears and apples)

The fan is the best shape for peaches, plums and figs grown against walls and may also be adopted for pears and apples, although the latter should not be grown against a wall (it is too hot a position for them) except in Scotland. The initial training is the same in each case although later pruning differs. Buying a ready-trained fan saves time but doing it yourself is more interesting and cheaper.

1   Plant a maiden against a southerly-facing wall and in early spring cut back either to a lateral or a bud about 60 cm (2 ft) high.

2   If there are any other laterals down the stem, cut them off flush with the stem.

3   As shoots develop choose two, one on each side of the stem and between 23 and 30 cm (9 and 12 in) high. Rub off all others below them.

4   When 45 cm (18 in) long, tie the selected shoots to canes fastened at 45 degrees to horizontal wires.

5   Cut out the central stem just above the upper side arm and protect the wound with bitumen paint. If the upper arm grown more strongly than the lower, temporarily depress it to a lower angle to slow down growth.

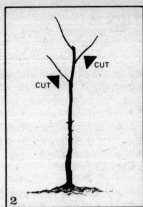

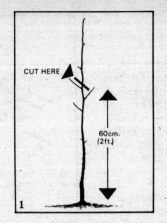

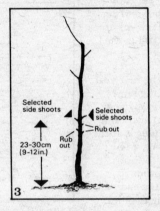

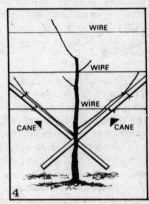

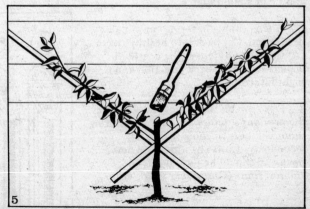

6 The next February (second winter) cut back each arm of the Y to a bud 30 to 45 cm (12 to 18 in) from the stem. Tie the resultant extension growth to the original canes. Look out for two more shoots above the branch and one beneath it, neither of those growing towards the wall or away from it. Rub off all other buds.

7 As these three additional shoots on each side grow long enough, tie them to canes fastened to the horizontal wires. Even the lower shoots must grow in an upward direction: if tied down to the horizontal, growth would almost cease.

8 In the third winter (February) prune all the ribs of the fan (branch leaders) back to about 66 cm (26 in). Again select two upper shoots and one lower to make new ribs of the fan. Rub out buds pointing at the wall or away from it. Subsequent pruning depends on the kind of fruit. With apples and pears each rib of the fan is treated like a cordon. For peaches and plums, see following pages.

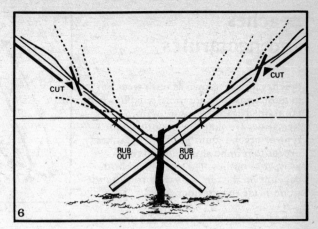

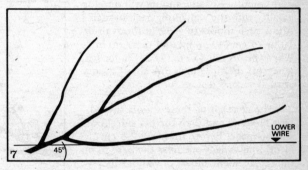

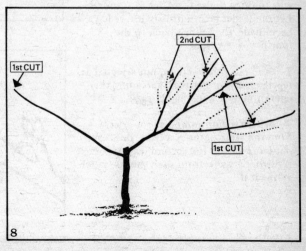

peaches and nectarines

Peaches may be grown as bush trees but in most areas they are more reliable when fan-trained against a sunny wall. Nectarines are simply a smooth-skinned type of peach requiring similar treatment except that in no situations do they prosper as bushes. The pruning of both depends on the fact that they fruit on the wood made the previous year.

1   At the stage reached on the previous page (picture 8) some shoots will develop parallel with the wall along each branch. Allow such shoots to grow at intervals of 10 to 15 cm (4 − 6 in) and tie them in. When they reach 45 cm (18 in) in length, pinch off the tip. Pinch unwanted shoots at their second leaf.

2   The next spring these shoots should bear blossom and then further sideshoots will be made. Before these are 2.5 cm (1 in) long, select one near the base to be the replacement shoot, one about half way to draw the sap and act as a reserve. Let the leader grow until six leaves have been made, then pinch back to the fourth.

3   Rub out other shoots, not selected as replacements or reserves, spreading this operation over a fortnight.

4   Where the unwanted shoot arises from the same point as a fruit, don't rub out but pinch at the second leaf. If there is further growth from such shoots, pinch at one leaf.

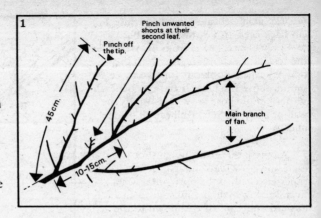

Pinch off the tip.

Pinch unwanted shoots at their second leaf.

45 cm.

10-15 cm.

Main branch of fan.

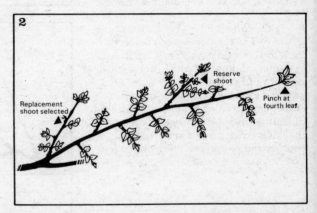

Replacement shoot selected

Reserve shoot

Pinch at fourth leaf.

5   After picking, cut each fruiting growth right back to its replacement shoot. Cut ties and refasten the replacements, spacing them evenly.

6   Peaches usually need thinning. Start when the fruitlets are the size of cobnuts, rubbing off the unwanted with finger and thumb. First take off those at the back of the branches.

7   Thin gradually over three weeks, next reducing all pairs to singles and eventually leaving the remaining fruit 23 cm (9 in) apart.

8   To assist ripening fasten back leaves shading the fruit or cut them off.

9   Peaches must be handled extremely gently so pick by lifting in the palm of the hand and twisting ever so slightly.

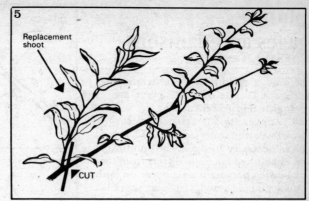

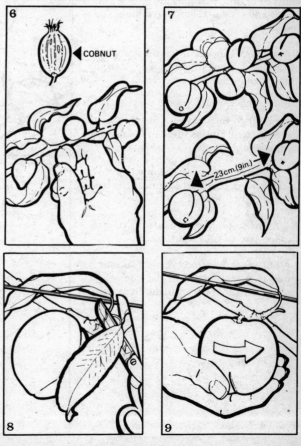

plums, gages and damsons

Because of the difficulties of tending tall trees and keeping off birds, plums are best grown in gardens as fans (see page 44) or pyramids. To restrict excessive growth root-pruning (see page 72) is often necessary for fans. The pruning of an established fan plum differs from that of a peach because fruit is borne on both young and old wood. Gages are special kinds of plums. Damsons are grown like plums and are suitable for pyramid training.

1   As shoots appear along the branches of the fan rub out promptly any pointing at the wall or directly away from it.

2   Pinch off the growing points of other laterals when they have six or seven leaves. Attend to this three or four times during summer.

3   In autumn cut back the pinched laterals either to a fruit bud near the base or to half their length.

4   Allow suitably placed laterals to grow as necessary to fill vacant spaces.

5   But never let strong vertical shoots grow, as they will steal all the tree's vigour. Cut them out or bend them over.

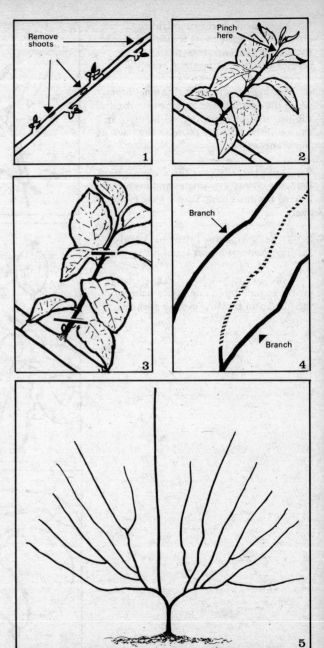

6 Pyramid plums cannot be bought: you must train your own. Buy a maiden on St Julien A rootstock and in early April cut back to 1.5 m (5 ft).

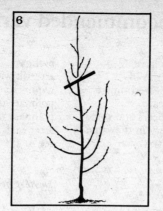

7 Cut off any sideshoots less than 46 cm (18 in) high and shorten others by a half.

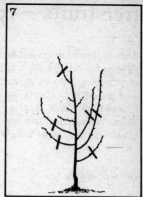

8 In the third week of July shorten the new extension growth of branches to 20 cm (8 in), cutting to a bud pointing down. Shorten laterals to 15 cm (6 in) but leave the central (vertical) leader alone. Repeat annually.

9 In April cut back the central leader by two-thirds of the growth made during the previous year.

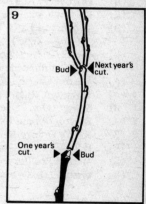

10 Repeat the April pruning annually until 2.7 m (9 ft) is reached, then wait until May and cut back the new growth to 2.5 cm (1 in) or even less. Repeat each May.

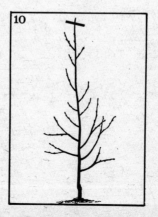

11 Should a strong vertical growth compete with the central leader, cut it out at source.

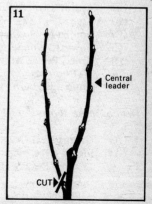

tree fruits — recommended varieties

The varieties recommended have been chosen for reliability. Varieties of outstanding flavour are indicated thus †. The letters in brackets indicate blossoming times. Apples, pears and some plums require another variety in the same blossom group with which to cross-pollinate. Varieties marked with an asterisk will not pollinate others and so require another in the same group to pollinate them and a third variety to pollinate that one. Season of use is given after each variety. For planting distances see p. 25.

Dessert apples

(A)	George Cave (Aug.—Sept.)
(B)	Discovery (Aug.—Sept.)
† (B)	Epicure (Aug.—Sept.)
(B)	Tydeman's Early Worcester (Aug.—Sept.)
(B)	James Grieve (Sept.—Oct.)
(A)	Lord Lambourne (Sept.—Nov.)
(A)	Merton Charm (Sept.—Nov.)
† (A)	Egremont Russet (Oct.—Dec.)
† (B)	Sunset (Oct.—Dec.)
†*(A)	Ribston Pippin (Nov.—Jan.)
† (B)	Kidd's Orange Red (Nov.—Jan.)
†*(B)	Holstein (Nov.—Jan.)
(B)	Merton Prolific (Nov.—Feb.)
*(B)	Crispin (Dec.—Feb.)

Cooking apples

(B)	Arthur Turner (July—Nov.)
(B)	Grenadier (Aug.—Sept.)
(C)	Golden Noble (Sept.—Jan.)
(C)	Howgate Wonder (Nov.—Feb.)
(C)	Lane's Prince Albert (Dec.—Mar.)
(C)	Annie Elizabeth (Dec.—May)

Dual-purpose apples

† (A)	George Neal (Aug.—Oct.)
(A)	Idared (Dec.—Apr.)
†	Crawley Beauty (Dec.—Mar.) (This flowers very late but pollinates itself.)

Dessert pears

†*(B)	Jargonelle (Aug.)
(B)	Williams' Bon Chretien (Sept.)
(C)	Gorham (Sept.—Oct.)
†*(B)	Merton Pride (Sept.)
† (C)	Onward (Sept.—Oct.)
*(C)	Bristol Cross (Sept.—Oct.)
(B)	Beurre Hardy (Oct.)
(A)	Louise Bonne of Jersey (Oct.)
(B)	Conference (Oct.—Nov.)
† (C)	Doyenne du Comice (Nov.—Dec.)
† (A)	Packham's Triumph (Nov.—Dec.)
† (C)	Glou Morceau (Dec.—Jan.)
† (B)	Joséphine de Malines (Dec.—Jan.)

Cooking pears

(C)	Improved Fertility (Sept.—Oct.)
*(C)	Catillac (Jan.—Apr.)

Acid cherries

Morello (Aug.—Sept.) Self-fertile.

Figs

White Marseilles (early)
Brown Turkey (mid-season)

Peaches
(For outdoor culture)

† Duke of York (July)
† Peregrine (early Aug.)
Rochester (mid-Aug.)

Nectarines

(For outdoor culture)

> Early Rivers (end July)
> † Humboldt (mid-Aug.)
> † Elruge (end Aug.)

Dessert plums and gages

† (A) Denniston's Superb (mid-Aug.)
† (A) Early Transparent Gage (mid-Aug.)
      Self-fertile.
  (C) Goldfinch (end Aug.)
† (C) Cambridge Gage (Aug.—Sept.)
† (A) Jefferson (early Sept.)
† (C) Kirke's Blue (early Sept.)
† (B) Count Althann's Gage
      (mid-Sept.)
  (A) Severn Cross (late Sept.)
      Self-fertile.
† (A) Coe's Golden Drop (Sept.—Oct.)

Cooking plums

  (A) River's Early Prolific (end July)
  (C) Czar (early Aug.) Self-fertile.

Dual-purpose plums

  (A) Early Laxton (end July)
  (C) Oullin's Gage (mid-Aug.)
      Self-fertile.
† (B) Victoria (mid-end Aug.)
      Self-fertile.
  (A) Warwickshire Drooper
      (mid-Sept.) Self-fertile.
  (C) Marjorie's Seedling
      (end Sept.) Self-fertile.

Damsons

  (B) Merryweather (Sept.)
      Self-fertile.

Note:
Self-fertile varieties will pollinate themselves and so a single tree may be grown. Others need another variety blossoming at the same time (as indicated by letters in brackets) but note that Jefferson and Coe's Golden Drop will *not* pollinate one another.

how to grow soft fruit

blackberries, loganberries and other hybrid berries

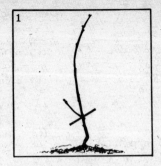

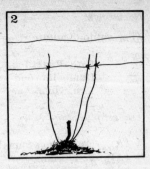

Blackberries and loganberries can often be grown in parts of the garden unsuited for other fruits. They will tolerate a fair amount of shade (and can therefore be trained against a north-facing wall) but do best in full sun and on a moisture-holding soil. Their vicious thorns used to be a drawback but now there are fruitful thornless varieties. Related hybrids may be grown in the same manner as blackberries.

1 After planting cut down to within 23 cm (9 in) of the ground.

2 In early spring apply a mulch to conserve moisture and tie in the new canes as they grow.

3 Blackberries and loganberries fruit on canes produced the previous summer and therefore in the second season the young canes will bear fruit. Immediately after picking cut down the old canes to soil level and tie in the new growths. Adopt a method of training which keeps the young canes above or separate from the old ones, thus avoiding disease infection by rain drip. Here is the fan method of training.

4 This is the alternate method of training: old growths to one side, new canes to the other.

5 Where lateral space is confined, the weaving system may be followed.

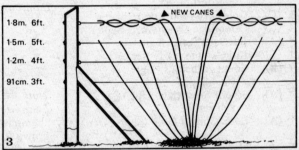

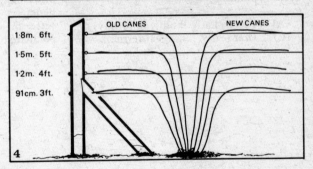

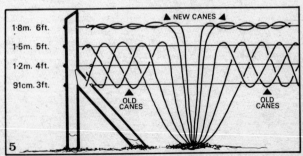

black currants

Rich in vitamin C, black currants are a valuable food and one of our highest yielding fruits. They need a well-drained but moisture-retentive soil. They will tolerate partial shade but do best in full sun. They are greedy feeders.

1   Start by buying 2-year-old bushes and planting them very slightly deeper than they were in the nursery.

2   Immediately after planting cut back every shoot to a bud less than 2.5 cm (1 in) above ground level.

3   Black currants fruit on old and young wood but more abundantly on the latter so pruning is aimed at stimulating new growth production. The first winter cut out only any weak growths. In subsequent years prune as soon as possible after picking, cutting out from one in four to one in three of all old shoots. The bush on the left is unpruned, that on the right pruned.

4   The pruning of black currants inevitably involves the sacrifice of some young wood at the tip of the old. Don't worry, but leave the remaining shoots at full length.

5   When picking don't attempt to remove black currants individually but take off each little bunch complete.

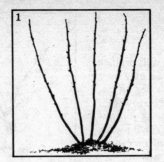

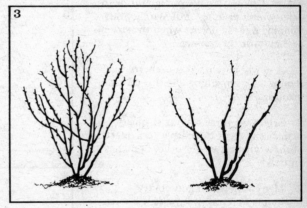

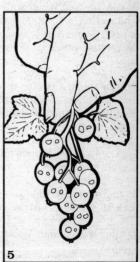

gooseberries

Gooseberries need a rich but well-drained soil and plenty of potash. They may be grown either as bushes — on a 'leg' of about 15 cm (6 in) to help keep lower branches clear of the soil — or as cordons, a productive way of utilising small pieces of wall or fence space. Birds often cause serious damage pecking the buds in winter. One way to discourage this is to defer winter pruning until March. Start thinning out the berries when the size of peas and use for cooking.

1   A newly purchased gooseberry bush should look something like this on planting.

2   Select the three or four strongest branches and cut these back to a quarter of their length. Cut out other branches entirely.

3   Many varieties of gooseberry (including Careless, Keepsake, Leveller, Warrington and Whinham's Industry) tend to have a drooping habit of growth, as here. To prevent branches trailing on the ground, prune to an upward-pointing bud.

4   For the first two or three winters, cut the main branch leaders back by half their length, more drastically if growth is weak.

5   Cut back weak branches and all laterals to one bud.

6   Between late June and mid-July cut back all sideshoots to the fifth leaf.

7   But leave branch leaders intact in summer.

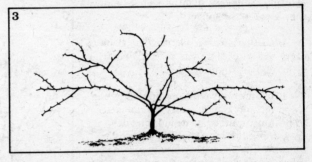

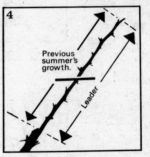

8 With older, established bushes, prune in winter to prevent branches crossing each other and to keep the centre of the bush open. Prune back some leaders hard to encourage new growth. Where old branches droop to the ground, as here, prune to a well-placed upward-pointing lateral to form a replacement branch.

9 Gooseberries may also be grown as single, double or treble-stemmed cordons or as fans and may then be trained against a wall or fence. Prune the arms of a fan as you would the main stem of a cordon.

10 In mid-June cut back all the laterals on a cordon to the fourth leaf.

11 In winter prune the previously cut laterals on cordons to the third bud. Cut back the leader by a third, provided you don't leave more than 25 cm (10 in) of new growth.

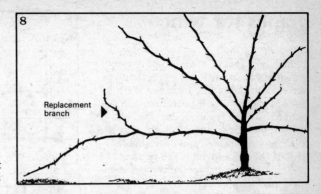

8

Replacement branch

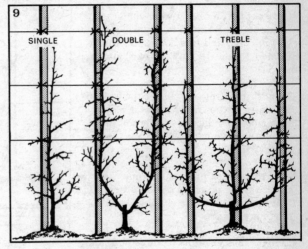

9

SINGLE   DOUBLE   TREBLE

10

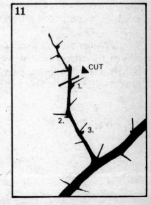

11

CUT
1.
2.   3.

grapes for wine

In Britain grapes of a wine-type may be grown outdoors with fair expectation of success south of a line from the Wash to Milford Haven. The location must be less than 61 m (200 ft) above sea level and the site sheltered and in full sun. The soil must be well-drained and only slightly acid. If the soil is deep it can be over chalk. Some wine grapes, although small, make excellent dessert.

1 To support a row of wine vines provide stakes 1.5 m (5 ft) high at 1.5 m (5 ft) intervals and two horizontal wires, 30 cm (1 ft) and 76 cm (2 ft 6 in) above the soil.

2 In spring plant one vine at the foot of each stake, at the same level as it was in the nursery as indicated by the soil mark on the stem, and cut down to less than 30 cm (1 ft).

3 In the first summer allow only one shoot to grow, pinching out all others. Tie loosely to the stake as soon as the growth is tall enough.

4 In November prune to three buds and allow three shoots to grow up, still pinching out all competitors.

5 In November of the second year tie two of the three shoots to the lowest horizontal wire, shortening each to 76 cm (2 ft 6 in). Cut the third shoot to three buds.

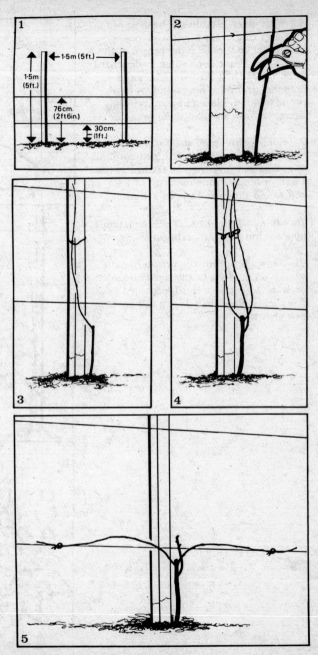

6 In the next summer allow three fruiting laterals to grow up from each arm and fasten to the higher wire. Tie in to the stake the three replacement growths, and pinch any laterals on these at one leaf.

7 When the berries start to swell, limit the bunches to two per vine the first season, in later years to from four to a maximum eight bunches per vine according to vigour.

8 After the removal of surplus bunches shorten sub-laterals to one leaf and cut back the fruiting laterals when they reach the top wire and at least one leaf beyond the top bunch.

9 Each autumn, immediately after leaf fall, cut the arms which bore the fruiting laterals and tie in one replacement on either side, limited to 76 cm (2 ft 6 in) in length, and cut back the third replacement shoot to three buds.

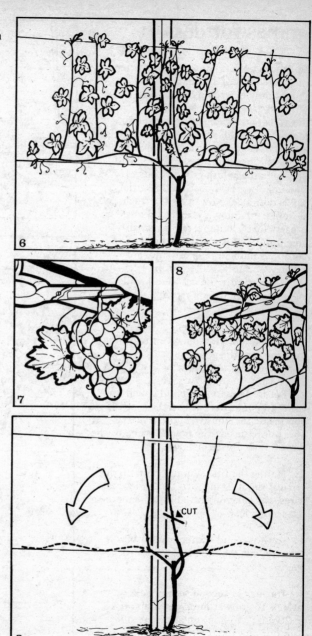

grapes for dessert

In Britain dessert grapes normally need the protection of a greenhouse and should only be grown outdoors in the warmest areas and most sheltered positions, preferably against a south-facing wall. In all cases good drainage is essential. Outdoors a soil of only average richness is best, for too rich a soil will only encourage lush growth and delay ripening. In greenhouse culture a richer soil is desirable. Nowadays the single rod system of training is usually followed and is particularly suitable for the small greenhouse. This may be likened to the cordon training of apples: vines are planted at intervals of 1.22 m (4 ft) and trained vertically up and then parallel to the roof, secured to horizontal wires 23 cm (9 in) from the glass.

1   Prepare a border outside the greenhouse and plant in autumn leading the cane into the greenhouse by removing a half-brick from the base.

2   Before January (to avoid bleeding) cut the young vine back to the second bud inside the house. If you have made up a border inside the house, prune to the second bud above soil level.

3   During the first summer train up one vertical shoot, tying it to the horizontal wires, and pinching off all other shoots at the second leaf.

4   In the second winter, always before January, cut the rod back to half its length.

5   During the second summer allow laterals to grow at intervals of about 18 to 20 cm (7 to 8 in) on alternate sides. Rub out unwanted growths as they appear.

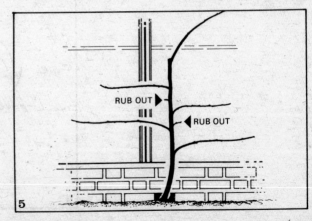

RUB OUT

RUB OUT

6   In this second summer a bunch or two or grapes may be permitted to develop. Pinch out fruiting shoots two leaves beyond the bunch and tie all laterals to the horizontal wires.

7   In the third winter again cut back the new leader growth of the vertical rod by a half and cut back all the laterals to two buds.

8   In spring if two shoots grow from one stub, rub out the weaker. Stop the main rod when it reaches the apex of the house. Stop fruiting laterals at two leaves beyond the bunch and non-fruiting laterals at the fourth leaf.

9   To attain good dessert size, the berries on the bunches will need to be thinned. Start when they are only 2.5 mm ($\frac{1}{10}$ in) in diameter, using sharp, pointed scissors and a little fork-ended stick to avoid fingering.

10   Continue thinning in easy stages so that by the time the process is complete the bunch will look rather 'thin' with the berries 2.5 cm (1 in) apart.

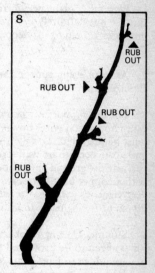

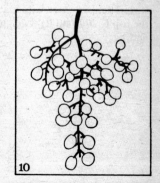

raspberries

This is an accommodating fruit which will grow almost anywhere. Raspberries will tolerate some shade but do best in sun and on a well-drained soil, slightly acid and rich in moisture-holding vegetable matter. Light, sandy soils need much watering and feeding. They are usually grown in rows, preferably running from south to north.

1   Preferably plant raspberries in autumn but definitely before April. Cover the roots 7.5 cm (3 in) deep and make firm.

2   After planting cut the canes down to about 25 cm (10 in).

3   For the support of the raspberry canes horizontal wires down the row must be provided. To take the strain the end posts need to be well strutted and the parts below ground should be treated with a copper-based preservative. For very vigorous varieties the wires should be 30 cm (1 ft) higher than indicated above.

4   Summer-fruiting raspberries (most kinds) need to be protected from birds. It is a good idea to have posts at least 46 cm (18 in) higher than the top supporting wire. Then, an extra wire is strained along the top to hold up lightweight plastic netting.

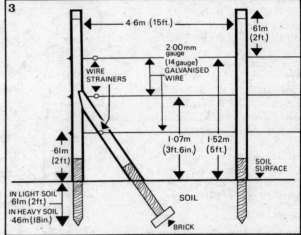

5 In sheltered gardens the easiest way to support raspberries is to supply double wires about 23 cm (9 in) apart and encourage the canes to grow up between these.

6 But the securest method of fastening, and necessary in windy places, is to tie each cane individually to the wire using soft string.

7 A time-saving way of tying the canes is to use a running string. Fasten one end to the end post and pass the ball of string round one cane and over the wire; then back past the cane and under the wire. Now slip the ball of string through the loop thus formed and pull reasonably tight.

8 When the picking of summer varieties · is finished (from the second summer onwards) cut the old canes down to soil level and tie in the best six of the new ones. Cut out the weaker canes completely. Autumn-fruiting varieties should not be cut down until February.

9 Towards the end of February tip the summer-fruiting canes, cutting them back to 15 cm (6 in) above the top wire. Autumn-fruiting canes tend to make shorter growth than the summer varieties and if overcrowded should be thinned out in early summer.

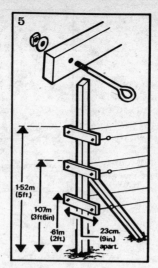

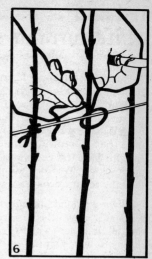

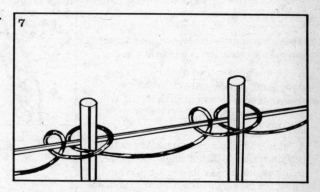

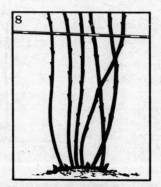

red and white currants

These are useful fruits, for they crop abundantly and start bearing at an early age (the first currants may be picked the summer after planting). The soil needs to be well-drained but should not be too rich. They will tolerate some shade. White currants have less eye-appeal for such purposes as jelly-making but are sweeter than the red for dessert.

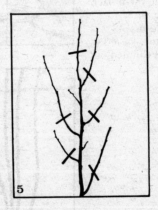
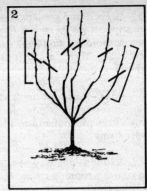

1   Plant a red currant bush at the same depth as it was in the nursery and cut back all branches to half their length, cutting to buds pointing outwards.

2   For the first three or four years cut back the new growth at the ends of the branches by a half. Subsequently only tip the leaders if growth is vigorous, pruning harder if stimulation is needed.

3   In summer, spreading the operation throughout June, cut back each new sideshoot growth to the fifth leaf. Then, in winter, further cut these shortened growths to the second bud.

4   Red and white currants adapt well to cordon training. Either single, double, treble or double-U cordons are useful forms for making use of narrow spaces on house walls or fences.

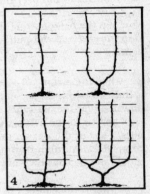

5   Just before the currants colour cut all new side growths to the fifth leaf and in winter cut back to the second bud. Cut back the new vertical extension growth by a third but never leaving more than 25 cm (10 in).

6   Red currants take a surprising time to reach full ripeness (and maximum sweetness) after they have turned colour and too many are picked before they are at their best.

strawberries

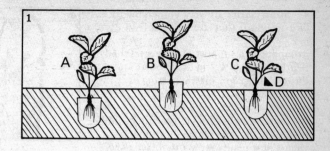

Probably most people's favourite soft fruit, strawberries may be grown in most districts. They do best in full sun on a well-drained medium soil rich in moisture-holding vegetable matter. Both heavy and very light soils will be improved by digging in farmyard manure or garden compost liberally. It is important that all weeds should be eliminated before planting. Three classes of strawberry are grown — the summer-fruiters (June–July), the perpetuals (June–October) and the alpines.

1 Summer-fruiting strawberries are best planted from late July to mid-September, as early as possible. If planted in spring remove the first summer's blossom to give the roots a chance to grow. Depth of planting is most important, in the examples above A is too deep, B is too shallow and C is correct. Spread out the roots and plant firmly but if the plants are in peat pots, soak in water for 10 minutes, don't remove from the pot and plant with the top of the pot D just level with the soil surface.

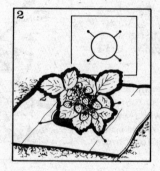

2 When the berries are swelling well (but not before this) litter the ground with straw to prevent soil splashing. As an alternative to straw you can buy strawberry mats and set one round each plant.

3 Or you can use a strip of black polythene, making a slit from the side to the middle opposite each plant. Tuck this under the fruit trusses and hold the edges down against the wind by covering with a little soil.

4   Strawberries are very vulnerable to bird attack. If they are not in a fruit cage,

extemporise a support of wire stretched tightly between 1.2 m (4 ft) posts and throw lightweight plastic netting over the whole row.

5   Most strawberries increase their kind by producing new plants on runners. Unless new plants are wanted (see page 71), cut off these runners as they show.

6   Immediately the last berry has been picked cut off all old leaves. Use shears at a height of 10 cm (4 in) so that new leaves are not harmed and remove straw, mats, plastic and all weeds.

7   Extra-early strawberries can be obtained in the greenhouse by rooting the first runners in small pots. When well rooted, sever and replant in larger pots, at least 15 cm (6 in) size, using John Innes potting compost.

8   Stand the pots in a sheltered spot, keep well watered and protect the pots from frost which might split them. In early January transfer to the lightest shelf in the unheated greenhouse.

9 Later a little gentle warmth can be given for the earliest fruit but this is not essential. Blossom must be pollinated by dabbing the centres with a wad of cotton wool.

10 Feed with liquid manure when the berries start to swell and prop the trusses up on bent pieces of wire. Jettison the greenhouse plants after fruiting.

11 Ripe strawberries may be picked several weeks earlier by covering first-year plants of an early variety with cloches or plastic tunnels in late February, in the South, in mid-March in the North. Follow the maker's instructions in erecting the plastic tunnel and on hot, sunny days open the tunnel wide, as here. In hot weather open cloches (if adjustable) or space them out with small gaps between.

12 Perpetual varieties should be planted in early autumn or spring and are grown in the same way as the summer kinds. Even if planted in the spring they may be allowed to fruit their first year provided all blossom showing in May is removed. Many growers always remove May blossom to avoid overlapping with the summer-fruiters and to secure a heavier crop later. The perpetuals' season may be extended into November by covering with cloches in early September and the plants should be cut down after fruiting.

13 A decorative and space-saving way of growing strawberries is in a barrel with 5 cm (2 in) diameter holes bored 15 cm (6 in) apart in the staves.

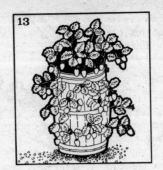
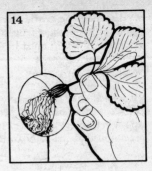

14 Place the plants in position through the holes as you fill the barrel firmly with a rich soil compost with plenty of rotting vegetable matter in it.

15 All strawberries need plenty of water during the growing season but barrels tend to dry out suddenly and so must be kept under constant observation.

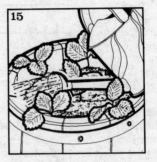

16 The protection of a strawberry barrel from the birds is easily contrived with a little ingenuity. As the berries hang down no strawing or mulching is necessary.

17 Alpine strawberries don't form runners and are raised from seed. Preferably sow under glass (10 to 16° C, 50 to 60° F) from January to March, and prick off the seedlings into another box as the first rough leaf stage is reached. Without heat sow under glass in April or outdoors in May.

18 In late May or early June plant alpine strawberry seedlings in their fruiting bed (rich soil, some shade an advantage), 30 cm (1 ft) apart and see they never want for water. Alpine strawberries hold their berries well up and so strawing is unnecessary.

soft fruits — recommended varieties

The varieties recommended have been chosen for reliability. Those of outstanding flavour are indicated with an asterisk. None of the soft fruits dealt with here require to be cross-pollinated and so it is quite practicable to grow a single specimen. For planting distances see page 26 .

Blackberries

Oregon Thornless*
Himalaya Giant (very vigorous, very spiny)

Loganberries

Thornless Loganberry

Other hybrid berries

Thornless Boysenberry*
Thornless Youngberry*

Black currants
(In order of ripening)
Boskoop Giant
Laxton's Giant
Tor Cross
Wellington XXX*
Baldwin (good, too, for deep freezing and richest in vitamin C)
Amos Black

Gooseberries

Green:
Keepsake (late, but first for picking green for cooking)
Lancer (late)

Red:
Whinham's Industry (mid-season)

White:
Whitesmith (early)
Careless (mid-season)

Yellow:
Leveller (mid-season)*

Grapes for wine
(Those marked 'd' are also good for dessert)

For white wine:
Riesling Sylvaner (d)
Siegerrebe (d)
Seyve-Villard 5/276
Madeleine Angevine 7972 (d)

For red wine:
Brant
Seibel 13053
Wrotham Pinot

Grapes for dessert
(For unheated greenhouses or sunny walls in the South)

Black:
Black Hamburgh

White:
Buckland Sweetwater
Royal Muscadine

(For heated greenhouses)
Black:
    Black Hamburgh
    Gros Colmar
    Madresfield Court

White:
    Muscat of Alexandria

Raspberries
(In order or ripening)

Summer-fruiting:
    Malling Promise
    Malling Jewel*
    Glen Clova
    Norfolk Giant

Autumn-fruiting:
    September
    Zeva

Red currants
(In order of ripening)
    Jonkheer van Tets
    Laxton's No. 1
    Red Lake
    Wilson's Longbunch

White currants
    White Versailles*

Strawberries

Summer-fruiting:
(In order of ripening)
    Cambridge Vigour (very early in
       first year, therafter mid-season)
    Cambridge Rival*
    Grandee (some berries of outsize
       in second year)*
    Royal Sovereign*
    Cambridge Favourite (heaviest
       cropper, very reliable but slight
       flavour)
    Talisman
    Domanil

Perpetual-fruiting:
    Gento

Alpine:
    Alexandria
    Delicious
    Baron Solemacher

fruit propagation

With the exception of melons and alpine strawberries, all the fruits normally grown in Britain are propagated vegetatively (by rooting cuttings or shoot tips or by grafting), raising from seed being adopted only to create new varieties. Budding (a form of grafting) is usually employed for tree fruits but this is work for the advanced amateur and outside the scope of this book. Soft fruits, however, are easily propagated.

1   For gooseberries and red and white currants, in late September or October cut shoots of the current year's growth which will be from 30 to 38 cm (12 to 15 in) long after the unripened wood towards the tip has been cut off.

2   From the red and white currant cuttings of ripened wood rub off all the growth buds except the top four.

3   The gooseberry cuttings (with all buds intact) should have their lower end dipped in a hormone rooting powder.

4   Black currant cuttings are taken at the same time but only about 23 cm (9 in) long after preparation. Remove no buds.

5   For planting soft fruit cuttings take out a narrow V-shaped slit trench 13 to 15 cm (5 to 6 in) deep and unless the soil is light sprinkle sand along the bottom.

6   Place the cuttings 15 to 20 cm (6 to 8 in) apart against the vertical side of the trench, replace the soil and press firm with the foot.

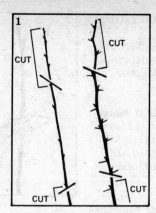

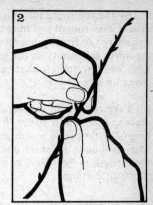

7 By the following autumn the cuttings should have rooted and may be transferred to fruiting quarters. Slice off the lower sideshoots on the gooseberries flush with the stem so that each plant grows on a 'leg'.

8 Take cuttings of grapevines at winter pruning time, 20 to 30 cm (8 to 12 in) long of well-ripened wood and each with four good buds. Plant outdoors to half their length in February, as with other soft fruit cuttings.

9 Grapevine cuttings are very vulnerable to cold spring winds. If in an exposed part of the garden, arrange a temporary shelter.

10 Grapevines may also be propagated from 'eyes'. Cut pieces of well-ripened wood 2.5 cm (1 in) long, each with one growth bud, and plant in John Innes potting compost with the bud exposed.

11 Stand the grapevine eyes in the greenhouse and start into growth in February at 21°C (70°F) and reduce by 6°C (10°F) when shoot growth begins.

12   Vines to be planted in the open must be gradually hardened to outdoor conditions by a spell in a cold frame.

13   Propagate only healthy, prolific strawberries. Remove the flowers, let the runners grow and peg down the rooting joints into good compost in small pots sunk in the ground.

14   Each runner can produce more than one new plant and each may be pegged down. Time is the limiting factor as new plants are wanted for planting out, ideally before the end of September.

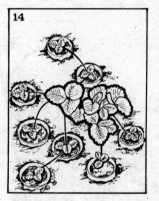

15   When the runners have rooted sever them from the parent plant and, a week later, plant out in fruiting quarters.

16   Blackberries, loganberries and other cane fruits are easily increased by layering. As the new shoots from healthy plants become long enough in summer, bend them over until 15 cm (6 in) of the tip can be buried in the soil. Make firm. Early the next spring sever the rooted tip from the parent and plant in fruiting quarters.

fruit trouble shooting

when trees won't fruit

Occasionally young fruit trees are reluctant to start cropping. Bearing in mind that if the tree is on a vigorous rootstock it will take longer than if on a dwarfing rootstock, try pruning less drastically. If growth is vigorous, reduce the nitrogen supply. Where this is of no avail, try bark ringing (for apples or pears) or root pruning. Where trees blossom but don't fruit, consider was frost responsible or is there no suitable pollinator?

1   In May, when other apples and pears are in flower, cut a ring in the bark round the trunk of the over-vigorous tree.

2   Make two parallel cuts 6 mm (¼ in) apart, just through the bark, no deeper. Peel off the bark between the cuts.

3   Immediately after cutting protect the wound from the air with a 2.5 cm (1 in) wide strip of insulating tape.

4   This tape should bridge the gap formed by the bark removal and not enter the wound.

5   In autumn when the wound has callused over, strip off the tape. Never bark ring stone fruits for fear of silver leaf disease infection.

6   For all stone fruits root pruning in early winter must be resorted to. You can dig up a young tree, prune the roots and replant.

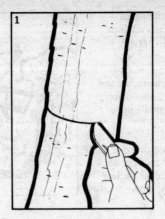

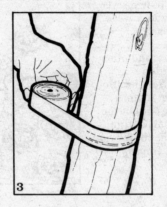

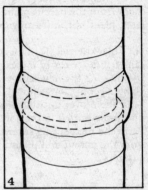

7 Older trees must be root pruned where they stand. Dig a two spade blades wide trench round the tree about 90 cm (3 ft) from the trunk and about 60 cm (2 ft) deep.

8 Saw through any thick roots so exposed but leave fibrous roots intact.

9 If you can find any tap roots under the tree, cut through them.

10 With older trees lessen the check by cutting a half-circle trench one year, doing the other half the next.

11 After root-pruning anchorage will be weak so see that the tree is soundly staked. Put down a moisture holding mulch in spring, avoiding the stem, and water liberally in dry summer weather.

12 Wall trees often have to be root-pruned to keep over-vigorous branches within the limits of the wall. Take out one trench 90 cm (3 ft) from the wall and two others at right angles to it and 75 cm (2 ft 6 in) from the stem.

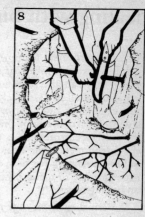

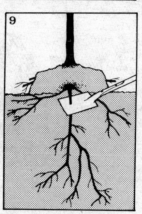

dealing with birds

Although birds help fruit growers by consuming vast numbers of insects, in the garden they can also be the most damaging of all pests, attacking ripening fruit in summer and pecking growth buds in winter, particularly of the soft fruits. The only sure protection is to cage the whole fruit plantation. Concrete and timber framework for such a cage can be made at home or metal supports can be purchased.

1   A permanent fruit cage may have sides of either plastic netting or wire netting, preferably of 13 mm (½ in) mesh, certainly no greater than 19 mm (¾ in). The roof should be of lightweight terylene or plastic netting removable in winter when snow threatens. Never use wire netting for the roof as rain-drip from it can be toxic. See that the door into the cage is wide enough to admit your wheelbarrow.

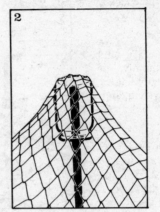

2   For temporary netting a glass jam jar inverted over the top of a supporting post will allow the netting to ride over easily without catching.

3   Small wall trees are easily protected with netting threaded over canes.

4   Black cotton may be twisted round branches as a temporary winter expedient but don't use nylon thread which does not break and can slice a bird's wing off. Far better is the black rayon web specially sold for this and quite large trees can be covered.

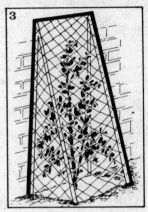

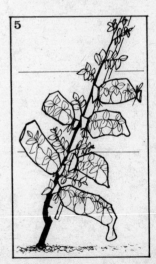

5   Individual fruit may be protected with muslin or plastic bags, the latter having small holes punched for ventilation. Sometimes whole branches can be protected with old stockings or tights.

spraying — safety rules and technique

Most of the fruit grower's troubles are caused by pests or diseases which can be checked and sometimes prevented or cured by spraying. Many of the substances employed are poisonous and must therefore be treated with caution, but if commonsense is used there is no cause for alarm.

1   Always keep spray materials under lock and key.

2   Wear old clothes for spraying and rubber gloves which can be washed afterwards.

3   Always follow maker's directions precisely and note carefully any safety interval which must elapse before crops are eaten.

4   Have measures, spoons etc. reserved for this purpose alone and wash immediately if a concentrated chemical touches the skin.

5   Stir diluted sprays thoroughly and when spraying occasionally shake the container to keep the spray well mixed.

6   Wash out old spray bottles and tins before consigning to the dustbin.

7   When spraying shield the eyes, preferably with goggles or at least with glasses.

8   Never attempt to spray (or apply a dust) in rain or very windy weather.

9   Don't spray in hot sunshine and on such days wait until late afternoon or early evening.

10   With winter washes hold the spray nozzle fairly close to the tree to give a thorough drenching.

11   With summer sprays a wetting of fine droplets is required and for this hold the sprayer or aerosol nozzle 30 cm (12 in) to 46 cm (18 in) away.

12   Direct the spray on the under surface of the leaves as well as on top.

13   Beware spray drift falling on edible crops due to be harvested in the near future.

14   To avoid harm to bees, the fruit-grower's best allies, never spray fruit trees or bushes in open flower.

15   When finished wash out the sprayer and any container used.

16   Never eat or smoke when spraying and conclude the operation by washing your face and hands.

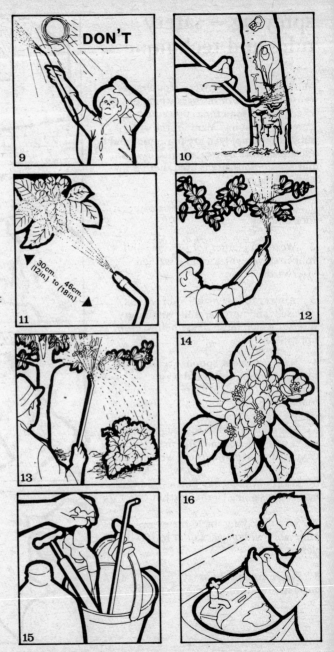

76

spray signals — blossom stages

The best time to apply many fruit sprays is dictated by the state of growth, not by the calendar. The blossom stages shown below are some of the most commonly used of these spray signals.

1 Apple. Bud burst.

2 Apple. Green cluster.

3 Apple. Pink bud.

4 Pear. Green cluster.

5 Pear. White bud.

6 Plum. White bud.

7 Plum. Cot split.

8 Black currant. Grape stage.

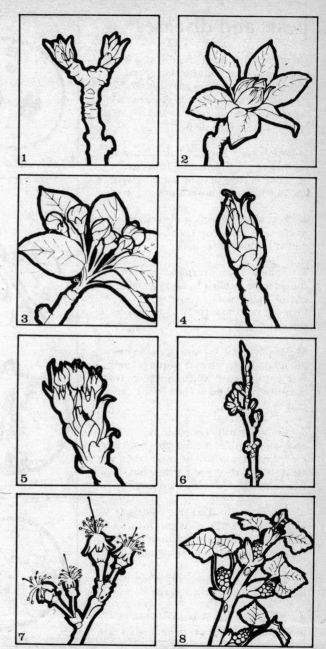

pests and diseases

There are many pests and diseases which might spoil your fruit but in general practice many of them are never seen. Here are the most obvious symptoms of the most common troubles and the steps to take in checking them.

1   Apple scab. Irregular, dirty brown patches on fruit caused by fungus. Scab-like blisters develop on shoots, olive brown patches on lower sides of leaves.

2   Pear scab. As with apple scab in severe cases fruit may crack. Other effects similar to those on apples.

3   Aphids. There are many kinds of aphid (some familiar to all as greenfly) and all fruits may be attacked. Often their sap sucking activity causes leaves to curl.

4   Woolly aphid or American blight. Found on apple trees. It protects itself with a white foam which looks like tufts of cotton wool and in time forms corky galls in the bark.

5   Codling moth. The moth lays it eggs on apples in June, the maggots bore into the fruit and may still be there when you eat it. If not, they make a hole out of the side from which a black mess exudes.

6   Apple sawfly. This lays its eggs at blossom time and the maggot makes a ribbon-like scare on the skin of the fruit. Attacked apples often fall prematurely.

7   Capsid bug. Causes corky bumps on apples and distorts their shape.

8   Bitter pit. A deficiency disease producing brown spots in an apple's skin and immediately beneath it.

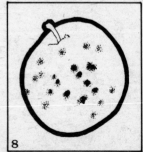

9   Winter moth. A group of moths which lay their eggs on fruit trees and these hatch out leaf and fruit-eating caterpillars.

10   Brown rot. A group of fungus diseases. Affected fruit turn brown and then either fall or become 'mummified' on the tree.

11   Silver leaf. A silvery sheen on the leaves is the most obvious symptom of this disease. All fruit trees can be affected but plums are the most common victims.

12   Peach leaf curl. This causes leaves to curl and pucker with blister-like swellings. Their colour turns from pale green to yellow, pink and red.

13   Strawberry botrytis. Also descriptively known as grey mould.

14   Black currant big bud. Abnormally precocious buds containing hundreds of minute mites.

15   Gooseberry sawfly caterpillars. These green creatures with black spots can soon defoliate a bush.

16   Gooseberry mildew. This fungus is common in damp, crowded garden conditions. Fruit and leaves may be spoiled.

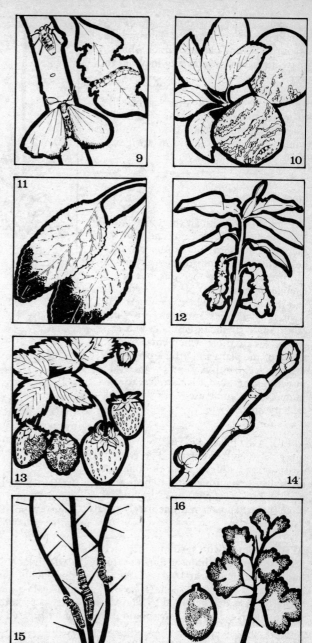

17   Mice. Long grass at the base of trees should never be allowed to remain. It is a favourite nesting place for mice which gnaw the bark in winter and may kill the tree.

18   Winter moths. As these cannot fly many may be trapped as they climb the trees by fastening grease bands round the trunk in October. Remove in April and burn.

Steps To Take

The golden rule with all spraying is to read the maker's directions and follow them exactly. Time and labour can often be saved by combining two or more sprays and applying together, but not all chemicals are compatible with each other and this should only be done where advised by the makers of the sprays in question. Systemic insecticides and fungicides are those which enter the tissue of the plant and attack pests and diseases from within. Derris is a useful insecticide because it is harmless to humans and can be used on fruit about to be harvested.

APPLE AND PEAR SCAB. To prevent, spray between bud burst and green cluster stage with captan or thiophanate-methyl systemic fungicide. Repeat at pink bud stage (apples) or white bud stage (pears) and again immediately petals have fallen.

APHIDS. Spray with systemic insecticide, fenitrothion, malathion or dimethoate at bud burst stage, repeat 14 days later and again later if aphids are seen. Over-wintering eggs will be killed by midwinter washing with tar oil but this should only be done once in every three or four years because it also destroys helpful insects.

BIG BUD. Spray with lime-sulphur at grape stage.

GOOSEBERRY SAWFLY. Spray with fenitrothion, malathion or derris soon after fruit sets.

GOOSEBERRY MILDEW. Spray with the systemic fungicides benomyl or thiophanate-methyl three times at 14 day intervals starting when first flowers open.

WOOLLY APHID. Spray as above (for aphids) and if patches of 'cotton wool' appear if possible apply spot treatment with a brush dipped in spray-strength insecticide.

CODLING MOTH. Spray fruits thoroughly with fenitrothion in mid June and again a month later. Reduce future attacks by trapping caterpillars in bands of corrugated cardboard or sacking tied round tree trunks in July and burned in December.

APPLE SAWFLY. Spray with systemic insecticide, fenitrothion or malathion immediately after petal fall. Spray plums at the cot split stage about 8 days after petal fall.

CAPSID BUG. Spray as for aphids at pink bud stage and at petal fall.

BITTER PIT. Review your management methods. Moisture shortage may be a cause and watering and mulching may help. Calcium deficiency may be a cause and can be rectified in future by spraying four times at 3 weekly intervals from mid-June with calcium nitrate dissolved in water at the rate of 170 g per 22 litre (6 oz per 5 gal).

WINTER MOTH. Spray apples and pears with fenitrothion at bud burst and repeat at green cluster stage. Also trap with grease bands, see picture 18.

BROWN ROT. Exercise strict garden hygiene, collecting all fallen fruit and picking rotting fruit off the tree and burning. Brown rot in store may be reduced by spraying with thiophanate-methyl in mid-August, repeating three weeks later.

SILVER LEAF. No cure. The disease enters through wounds and so pruning of stone fruits should be done when the disease is least active, in spring, summer or very early autumn. Cut out all silvery foliage, cutting back 15 cm (6 in) beyond the point where the brown stain within the wood ceases, covering all wounds with protective tree paint.

PEACH LEAF CURL. Spray with lime sulphur, liquid copper fungicide or captan in January, repeating 14 days later. Spray again in autumn just before the leaves fall.

STRAWBERRY BOTRYTIS. Prevent by spraying with thiophanate-methyl three times at 14 day intervals starting when first flowers appear.

miscellaneous fruit operations

harvesting and storing

If fruits are to taste their best they must be picked at the right moment. All soft fruits are sweetest and possess most flavour when left on the plant as long as possible, until fully coloured and absolutely ripe. In the case of apples and pears picking time has considerable bearing on subsequent keeping quality.

1   Never pick apple or pear which does not part quite readily from the spur, retaining the stalk on the fruit.

2   Pick early pears as soon as the green ground colour begins to pale and before it has turned yellow.

3   Shrivelling in store is commonly the result of premature picking although too warm and too dry conditions can also contribute to this.

4   Pick apples and pears by lifting them in the palm of the hand and then giving a very slight twist. Never hold with the finger tips.

5   Handle the fruit as gently as eggs. Never tip them from one container to another — place them there — and line the bucket or basket with something soft.

6   The colouring of keeping apples can be deepened by laying the fruit on a double thickness of newspaper spread on the lawn for three weeks. Protect from birds.

7   Late keeping apples to be stored on shelving are best individually wrapped. Lay the apple at the centre of the wrap . .

8   . . . and fold over two opposite corners of the wrap. Use the specially made oiled apple wraps or squares of newspaper.

9   Fold over the other two corners of the wrap, making no attempt to twist them together.

10   Hold the ends in place by inverting the wrapped apple on its storage shelf.

11   Apples can also be kept in polythene bags. Put not more than 1.8 kg (4 lb), all of the same variety, in a bag, and seal the top with the usual metal twist.

12   A little ventilation inside the bag is essential, however. To provide this, cut a small piece off each corner of the bag.

13   Don't wrap or bag keeping pears but lay out on shelving so that the fruits don't touch one another.

14   The ideal fruit store is cool, dark, well ventilated and slightly damp. Cellars are ideal. Damp down outhouse floors occasionally.

15   Apples and pears will only keep well until their natural eating season. Take pears into a warm room three or four days before required for dessert.

16   Inspect stored fruit regularly and remove decaying specimens. Watch for mice and rats and take steps to prevent their depredations.

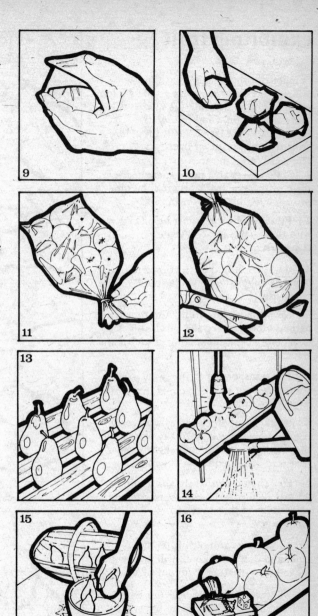

exhibiting fruit

Competitive showing is great fun, bringing the spice of rivalry to the garden routine. The golden rule for success is to study the schedule and follow its provisions to the letter. Fruit should be properly ripe but never overripe.
The word 'dish' in the schedule covers any appropriate dish, plate or receptacle. Plates are sometimes provided by the show organisers.

1   Fruit for showing must be picked with their stalks intact, even on raspberries.

2   Currants should be in complete bunches unless the schedule stipulates otherwise.

3   Never polish any fruit. Aim to leave natural bloom intact and this involves remarkably careful handling of plums and grapes.

4   For transporting to the show pack fruit on a layer of tissue paper in a cotton wool lined box.

5   In staging apples and pears place all but one round the edge of the plate and then raise the central fruit slightly on a neat wad of folded tissue paper.

6   Size should be slightly above the normal average but evenness of size and uniformity of shape are of first importance.

7   Avoid spots and blemishes of any kind, and don't think you will hoodwink the judge by putting them out of sight.

8   Wherever possible label your fruit with the name of the variety but write nothing else on the card.

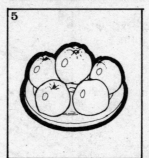

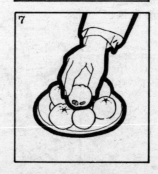
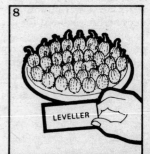

how to grow melons

Although fruits, melons are raised from seed and grown like vegetables. Where a night temperature of 16° C (60° F) can be assured, seed may be sown in the greenhouse in January. For subsequent cold frame or cloche culture sow seed in heat in early April. Only in the warmest areas may melons be started in warmth and, in a gamble with the weather, be transferred to the open ground. Recommended varieties: for the heated greenhouse, Hero of Lockinge, Blenheim Orange; for unheated houses, cold frames or cloches, Charentais, No Name, Ogen; hardiest of all for frames, cloches or open, Sweetheart.

1   Sow melon seeds on their sides 2 cm (¾ in) deep in moist compost in 7.5 cm (3 in) pots and place in a heated propagator, a temperature of 18 to 21° C (65—70° F) being desirable.

2   Failing a propagator, plunge the pots in a box of moist peat, cover with glass and newspaper, and stand over the heating pipes or tubes in the greenhouse.

3   When the seedlings show remove to the lightest part of the greenhouse. Plant out when four rough-edged leaves have grown.

4   In the greenhouse plant on mounds in rich, porous soil. Stop the main shoot at 1.8 m (6 ft) and pinch laterals when 30 cm (1 ft) long.

5   Hand pollinate female flowers with the pollen laden centre of a male flower. All on one plant must be fertilised on the same day.

6   Take the weight of developing greenhouse fruit by supporting them with slings of netting.

7 In cold frames set two plants in opposite corners. With cold frame or cloche plants pinch at the fifth leaf, select the best two of resultant sideshoots and pinch out others. Stop these two shoots when 40 cm (16 in) long and when fruit have set pinch two leaves beyond.

feeding fruit

The feeding of both tree and soft fruits is probably the most difficult problem the grower has to face. Each kind of fruit has different requirements; even varieties of the same fruit can differ in their needs. The grower must keep a close eye on growth and feed accordingly. The suggestions given in the tables below are for straight fertilisers but in practice many gardeners like to use proprietary mixtures and preparations of organic manures and in such cases the gardener must try to evaluate them by comparing the analysis given on the bag or package with the proportions suggested below. Proprietary fertilisers intended for roses are often very suitable for fruit. For tree fruits nitrogen (N) is best applied in late January or early February, phosphorus (P) and potassium (K) whenever convenient in winter or early spring. For soft fruits give nitrogen in February or early March, phosphorus and potassium at any time in winter or early spring.

| FRUIT | FERTILISER TO APPLY | ANNUAL APPLICATION | | REMARKS |
		g per sq m	oz per sq yd	
APPLES	Sulphate of ammonia (nitrogenous)	35	1	To trees in grass give half as much again. Cooking apples need rather more nitrogen than dessert kinds.
	Sulphate of potash (potassic)	18	½	If leaf scorch symptoms of potash deficiency appear, increase by up to 4 times.
	Superphosphate (phosphatic)	35 to 70	1 to 2	Every 2 or 3 years only.
	Magnesium sulphate (Epsom salts)	35 to 70	1 to 2	

FRUIT	FERTILISER TO APPLY	ANNUAL APPLICATION		REMARKS
		g per sq m	oz per sq yd	
PEARS	Sulphate of ammonia	35	1	To trees in grass half as much again.
	Sulphate of potash	18	½	
	Superphosphate	35 to 70	1 to 2	Every 2 or 3 years.
	Rotted farmyard manure or garden compost.	Wheelbarrow load per 6 sq m (8 sq yd)		Apply in spring.
CHERRIES	Rotted farmyard manure or garden compost	As for pears		
	Sulphate of potash	35 to 53	½ to ¾	
	Superphosphate	70 to 100	2 to 3	Every 2 or 3 years.
FIGS	No feeding necessary in first 5 years. Thereafter a light spring mulch of rotted manure or garden compost.			
PEACHES & NECTARINES	Light mulch of rotted manure or compost in May. Too much feeding may cause excessive growth and reduce fruiting.			
PLUMS, GAGES & DAMSONS	Sulphate of ammonia	18 to 27	½ to ¾	
	Sulphate of potash	18	½	
	Superphosphate	53 to 70	1½ to 2	Every 2 or 3 years.
	Light mulch of rotted manure or compost in April.			
BLACKBERRIES, LOGANBERRIES & OTHER HYBRIDS	Mulch well in spring with rotted manure or garden compost. Failing that, sulphate of ammonia	70	2	Apply in spring
	Sulphate of potash	27	¾	Apply in March
BLACK CURRANTS	Mulch in spring with rotted manure or compost, 1 wheelbarrow load per 6 sq m (8 sq yd) plus — sulphate of ammonia	35	1	
	Sulphate of potash	12	1/3	
	Superphosphate	35	1	

FRUIT	FERTILISER TO APPLY	ANNUAL APPLICATION		REMARKS
		g per sq m	oz per sq yd	
GOOSEBERRIES	Mulch during winter with manure or compost as for black currants plus — sulphate of potash	27	¾	
GRAPES, outdoors	Mulch in early summer with rotted manure or compost. Fork in during winter. Supplement with mixed fertiliser at 70 g per sq m (2 oz per sq yd).			
GRAPES, under glass	Immediately after flowering dress border with special vine fertiliser 70 g per sq m (2 oz per sq yd) and liberal mulch of well-rotted manure or compost.			
RASPBERRIES	As for blackberries			
RED & WHITE CURRANTS	Sulphate of ammonia	35	1	
	Sulphate of potash	12 to 18	1/3 to ½	
	Superphosphate	35	1	
STRAWBERRIES	Sulphate of potash	18	½	Lightly fork in after cleaning up after fruiting.

preparing for vegetables

planning a crop rotation

To ensure that the area devoted to vegetables will make its maximum contribution to the family's health and the domestic budget, most careful planning is essential. No land should be left unnecessarily idle yet always a plot must be available to take seedlings raised in a seedbed or under glass. To avoid gluts and shortages, sowings must be made in sequence and with one eye to when the crops should mature. Allocate a relatively small part of the vegetable garden to the so called permanent crops which occupy the ground for a number of years and for the short term crops work out a rotation as suggested below.

1   This is a three year rotation plan for the vegetable garden. Each year the crops advance one plot. Thus, in the second year the plot 2 crops go into plot 1 and those in plot 3 move to plot 2 while plot 1 crops rotate to plot 3. This scheme makes the fullest use of the plant foods in the soil and helps to starve out pests and diseases which are deprived of a suitable host. Onions are often grown on the same plot each year and in this case a permanent fourth plot must be allocated to them.

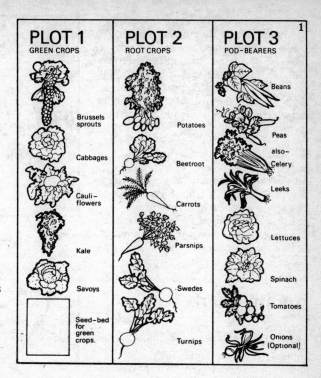

PLOT 1 GREEN CROPS — Brussels sprouts, Cabbages, Cauliflowers, Kale, Savoys, Seed-bed for green crops.

PLOT 2 ROOT CROPS — Potatoes, Beetroot, Carrots, Parsnips, Swedes, Turnips.

PLOT 3 POD-BEARERS — Beans, Peas also—Celery, Leeks, Lettuces, Spinach, Tomatoes, Onions (Optional)

1

2   Intercropping is a device for securing maximum output by growing a small, quick-maturing crop between the rows of larger, slower crops. Examples are lettuce, radishes, summer spinach, summer turnips or shorthorn carrots, as here, sown between the rows of peas or runner beans. The intercrop is ready before the major crop is fully grown.

3   Catch cropping is another space saving idea and consists of obtaining a quick crop from ground being held in readiness for a later crop. Examples of this are to plant early lettuce or sow radishes along the sides of celery trenches in spring. These crops will be finished before the celery is planted out in June.

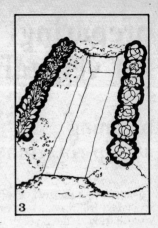

sowing seeds

Vegetable seeds may be sown in pots, boxes or other containers for raising under cover or, outdoors, in a special seed bed or direct in the bed where the crop is to mature. When sowing in containers one should use a sterilised compost, thus eliminating pests, diseases and competing weed seeds. The ordinary gardener has the choice of buying a sowing compost made up to the John Innes formula or one of the proprietary soilless composts. In the latter case the maker's direction should be obeyed precisely. With John Innes compost the following procedure applies.

1   When using a wooden seed box cover the drainage spaces in the bottom with clean pieces of broken pot or tile.

2   Fill the seed box (or pot) loosely with the sowing compost.

3   Firm round the edges with the finger tips.

4   Strike off the surplus level with the top of the container.

5   With a block of wood press down the compost evenly so that its surface is 1.25 cm (½ in) below the edge.

6   When preparing a pot for sowing firm the compost with the base of another pot.

7   Water thoroughly with a fine rosed can and leave for some hours for the moisture to seep evenly through the compost.

8   Next, make shallow depressions (called drills) in the compost surface, using a piece of cane cut to the appropriate length.

9   To sow thinly, fold a piece of stiff paper in half, put some seed in the fold and tap gently as you move the paper over the drill.

10   Sift a little fairly dry compost over the seeds to cover them. Small seeds need a very light covering, large seeds about 0.5 cm (¼ in).

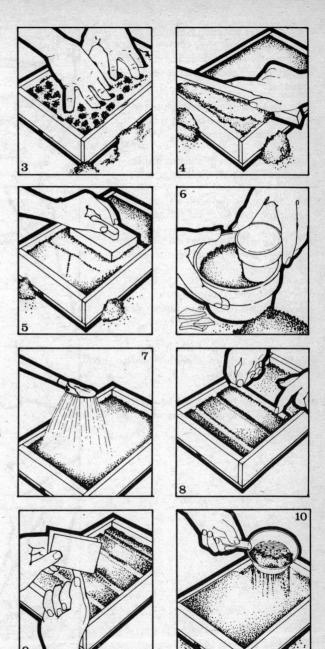

11 Further watering is usually unnecessary until after germination. When watering is required, dip the container in water and let it seep upwards.

12 To prevent evaporation before the seedlings emerge, cover the box or pot with a sheet of glass.

13 Alternatively place the whole container in a polythene bag.

14 Shade the top with a sheet of newspaper laid flat over the surface.

15 The very moment you first see seedlings have broken the surface, remove all covering.

16 Outdoors, the seedbed must be broken down finely. Seedlings will not grow well among clods of earth.

17 Start by lightly forking over the surface breaking up larger lumps with the tines of the fork.

18 Now the lumps must be pulverised even more. You can do this with a garden roller.

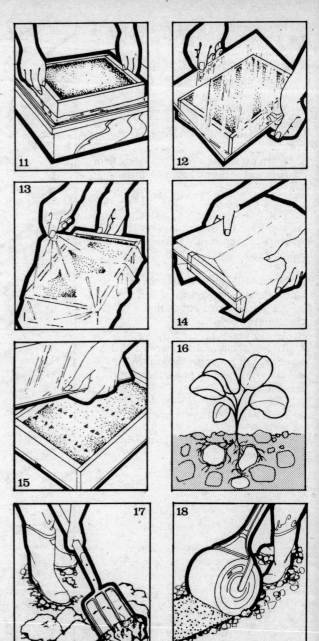

19 Or you can tread over the bed, moving gradually over it with a shuffling movement.

20 Rake over the bed to remove surface stones.

21 Then rake first in one direction and then at right angles until the soil is quite fine.

22 In this raking hold the handle of the rake at a low angle.

23 If the rake is held at a steep angle to the ground, the surface is liable to become wavy instead of level.

24 With the garden line mark where each row of seeds is to be sown.

25 Along the line make a shallow drill by pressing the rake handle into the soil.

26 Or use the head of the rake to make this depression.

27 Alternatively, and desirable for deeper drills, draw the hoe blade along the line.

28 Various devices are on the market to aid thin sowing. Some gardeners like to use one of these.

29 Others prefer to sow direct from the packet, tapping this gently as it is drawn along the drill.

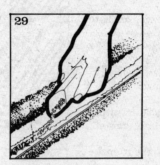

30 With some seeds, thin sowing is achieved most easily by taking a pinch in the fingers and distributing it along the drill.

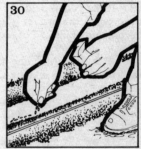

31 Cover the seeds by raking gently.

32 Don't forget to mark the row before putting away the garden line.

using frames, cloches and tunnels

Although excellent vegetables may be grown without the aid of any form of artificial protection, cold frames, cloches and plastic tunnels are an invaluable investment. With their aid crops can be started earlier in the season and, in some instances, continued later. The raising of seedlings is often made easier and some crops may be grown which otherwise would be impossible or a sheer gamble with the weather.

1   Cold frames and cloches are available in almost infinite variety, some in glass, others plastic. Although initially more expensive, glass cloches are preferable because they imprison heat, as does a glasshouse. Plastic cloches and tunnels are not to be despised, however, as they bring crops on by protecting them from cold winds and keeping off marginal frosts.

2   Cold frames are essentially miniature greenhouses. They are usually static with a permanent foundation as here.

3   Mobile frames can be taken from one crop to another as required.

4   Dutch lights are single sheets of framed glass about 1½ m x 80 cm (59 x 31½ in) which are supported on temporary or permanent wooden supports.

5   Very small cloches, such as the tent pattern seen here, are cheaper to buy but only useful for raising seedlings or low crops such as radishes.

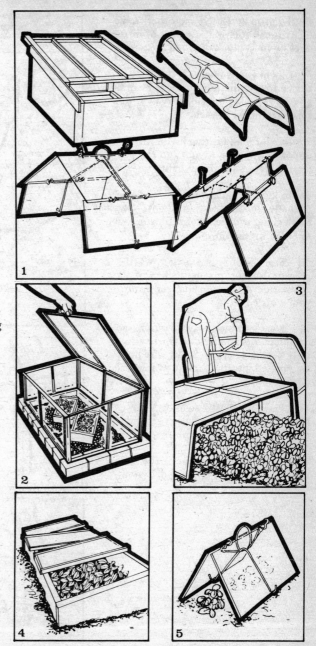

6   To prop up Dutch and other frame lights for ventilation, use pots of different sizes or cut a block of wood in steps.

7   Cloches are sometimes made with a device for ventilation. If not, air can be given by spacing the cloches out with a small gap between each.

8   In winter and spring it is most important to keep frames and cloches clean to let in maximum light.

9   In high summer it may be necessary to shade cloches and frame lights. Do this by flecking with whitewash, just enough to break up the sunshine.

10   Seal the ends of cloche rows to prevent draught, placing a sheet of glass or plastic over the opening and securing with a cane.

11   Plastic tunnels may be purchased in complete kits and used to start various early vegetable crops. Stout wire hoops are pressed into the ground at intervals down the row.

12   Place the plastic strip over these hoops and hold down with a second set of hoops which clip to the first.

13   Fasten the polythene at the end of the row by tying it to a peg driven into the ground.

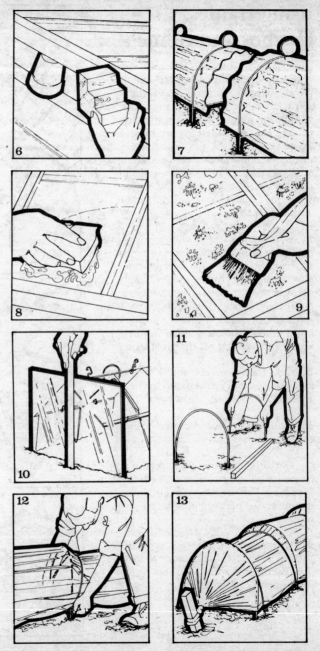

how to grow vegetables

the green crops

Broadly speaking all the green crops need similar treatment. Required to make plenty of leaf growth, they need rich soil, deeply dug. Dig well in advance so that the ground has settled by planting time. The greens to stand the winter (late cauliflowers, savoys, kales, sprouting broccoli and spring cabbage) should not have as rich soil as the others and where convenient may follow another crop for which the ground was well manured. The green crops prefer slightly alkaline soil. Never mix lime with manure or fertilisers but scatter it over the soil surface after digging.

1   Raise all the members of the brassica (cabbage) family shown above by sowing in a seedbed outdoors and transplanting later to their final quarters. *A* spring cabbage, *B* summer cabbage, *C* Savoy cabbage, *D* red cabbage, *E* cauliflower, *F* green sprouting broccoli (calabrese), *G* white or purple sprouting broccoli, *H* Brussels sprouts.

2   The earliest summer cauliflowers are an exception: they need to be sown in February in a warm greenhouse.

3   In March harden off these early cauliflower seedlings with a spell in a cold frame and then plant outdoors.

4   The bed for raising the cabbage family seedlings need not be large — say 1 m (1 yd) wide by 2 or 3 m (or 2 to 3 yd) long will be ample. For a year-round programme, many sowings

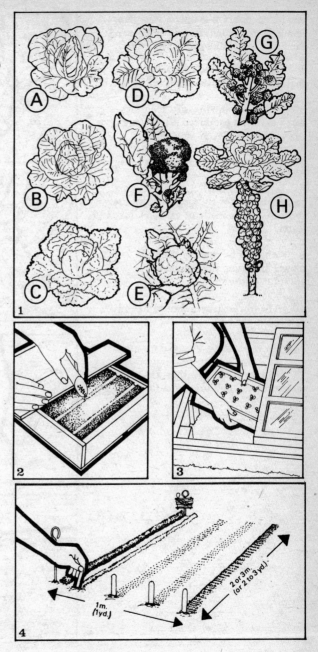

will be necessary but only a few plants required from each. Sow in short rows, therefore, and label each carefully.

5   Thin out the seedlings as necessary so that no two touch one another.

6   Transplant the brassica seedlings when each has produced 4 or 5 true (rough-edged) leaves.

7   Use a handfork to lift the seedlings.

8   To guard against club root disease and cabbage root fly maggots, dip the roots in a paste made of calomel dust and water.

9   Plant firmly, making the hole with a trowel and using the handle to consolidate the soil.

10   The lowest leaves should be only just above the soil.

11   After planting, give some water.

12   In very sunny weather, try to arrange some temporary shading.

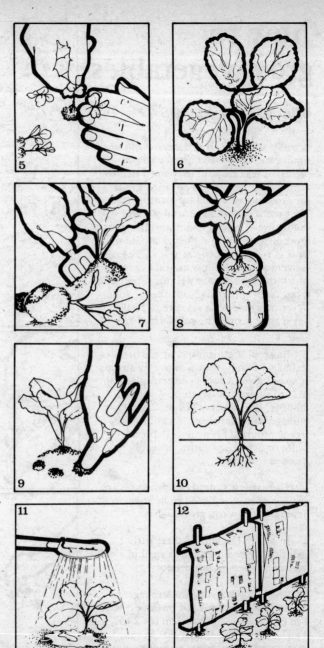

13   Birds often attack brassica seedlings. Strips of wire netting with 13 mm (½ in) mesh, laid along rows, are one way to protect them.

14   As cauliflowers and Brussels sprouts grow, hoe a little soil up to the stems to give support.

15   In windy gardens, stake Brussels sprouts individually or run a string down the row to which each can be tied.

16   Summer sunshine can discolour the curds of cauliflower. Prevent this by bending a leaf over the centre.

17   Protect winter cauliflower (broccoli) from frost as in frame 16. On exposed sites heel the plants over away from icy winds.

18   When Brussels sprouts are ready, start picking from the bottom and work up the stem.

19   Plant spring cabbages at half the final distance in the row. Then in early spring use alternate plants as 'spring greens' leaving the remainder room to mature fully.

20   Chinese cabbage looks rather like a Cos lettuce and may be eaten raw or cooked. Mid-ribs may be cooked separately and eaten like asparagus. Sow where they are to mature and never transplant.

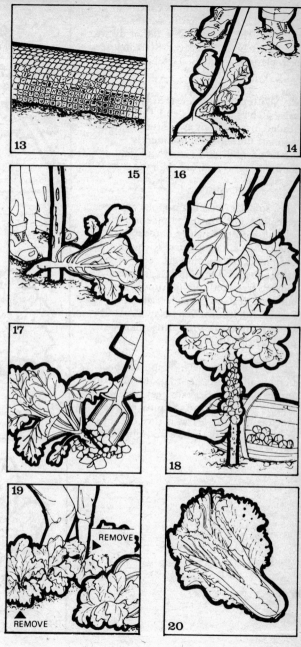

21   The kales (sometimes called borecole) are a very hardy winter standby. The Scotch kales, tall or dwarf, have densely curled leaves. Start in a seed bed, planting in final quarters in July or early August.

22   With the smooth-leaved types of kale, such as Cottager's and Thousand-headed, use the tops as winter greens and then cut the shoots subsequently produced while still young and tender. Kales need less rich soil than other brassicas.

23   Spinach (left) is a popular summer vegetable. For continued pickings sow several small fortnightly batches in drills where they are to mature. Rich, deep soil and plenty of moisture are required. On lighter soils and in hot, dry summers spinach frequently bolts (runs to seed) but New Zealand spinach (right) thrives in such conditions. Start New Zealand spinach under glass in spring, plant outdoors in late May.

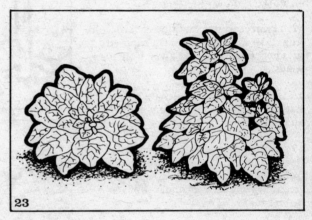

24   Perpetual spinach or spinach beet (left) is another easier-to-grow substitute for real spinach. Seakale beet (right) may also be grown instead of spinach. The green part of the leaves is torn off for use as spinach and the white mid-ribs cooked like seakale.

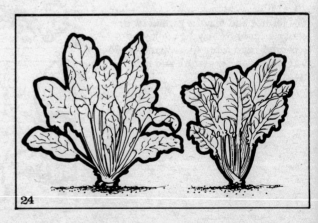

the green crops — recommended varieties

KEY: A = Sow where crop is to mature
         B = Sow in a seedbed, transplant later
         C = Sow under glass, in heat

CROP and recommended varieties	When to sow	Where to sow	Final spacing				When ready
			Between rows cm	in	In the row cm	in	
CABBAGE — spring Hispi, Flower of Spring, Wheeler's Imperial	July— Aug	B	45	18	45	18	Spring
CABBAGE — summer Hispi Greyhound Winnigstadt	Mar— Apr	B	45	18	45	18	June June—July Aug—Oct
CABBAGE — autumn-winter, Christmas Drumhead	May	B	60	24	45	18	Late autumn
CABBAGE — Savoy Best of All January King Rearguard	May	B	60	24	45	18	Oct—Nov Nov—Jan Dec—Apr
CABBAGE — red Blood Red Ruby Ball	Mar— Apr	B	60	24	45	18	Autumn
CABBAGE — Chinese Sampan Nagaoka	June— July	A	45	18	23	9	Sept—Oct
CAULIFLOWER— Summer All the Year Round	Feb	C	60	24	45	18	June
All the Year Round	Mar— Apr	B					July—Sep

CROP and recommended varieties	When to sow	Where to sow	Between rows cm	in	In the row cm	in	When ready
CAULIFLOWER—							
autumn							
Bondi	late	B	76	30	60	24	Sep
Kangaroo	Apr to						Sep—Oct
South Pacific	mid—						Oct
Snowcap	May						Nov—Dec
CAULIFLOWER—	Apr—	B	60	24	60	24	
winter	May						
(broccoli)							
Superb Early							Jan—Feb
White							
St. George							Mar—Apr
English							Apr
Winter							
SPROUTING BROCCOLI							
Green (Calabrese)							
	Mar—May	B	60	24	45	18	
Express Corona							Aug—Sep
Green Comet							Aug—Sep
Late Corona							Sep—Nov
White, Early	Apr	B	60	24	60	24	Mar—Apr
White, Late	May	B	60	24	60	24	Apr—May
Purple, Early	Apr	B	60	24	60	24	Mar—Apr
Purple, Late	May	B	60	24	60	24	Apr—May
BRUSSELS SPROUTS	mid Mar—	B	76	30	60	24	
Peer Gynt	mid Apr						Oct—Dec
King Arthur							Nov—Dec
Prince Askold							Dec—Jan
Fasolt							Dec—Feb
KALE (Borecole)	Apr—	B	60	24	60	24	Mar—May
Scotch curled:	May						
Pentland Brig							
Dwarf Curled							
Tall Curled							
Cottager's							
Thousand-headed							
SPINACH BEET	Apr—	A	30	12	30	12	Summer
(Perpetual-	July	A	30	12	30	12	Winter and
spinach)							spring
No varieties							
SEAKALE BEET	Apr—	A	45	18	23	9	Jun—Oct
No varieties	Aug	A	45	18	23	9	Spring

potatoes

Some gardeners used to feel they had insufficient space for potatoes and, because they were so cheap in the shops, thought them hardly worth growing anyway. Now the cheap food days are past and new potatoes early in the season are an expensive luxury. Every gardener should try at least to find room for a few earlies, planting them in March. Mid-season and maincrop varieties are planted in April.

1   During the winter, unless the previous crop was well manured, dig farmyard or stable manure liberally into ground intended for potatoes.

2   Near planting time, work in a dressing of a general garden fertiliser at the rate of 105 g per sq m (3 oz per sq yd).

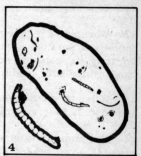

3   Potatoes are often planted as a first crop on ex-grassland. Such ground is usually full of wireworms. Fortunately earlies are unlikely to be attacked.

4   You can clear wireworm-infested soil by dusting with Gamma BHC powder but must not grow potatoes there for 18 months.

5   It pays to sprout seed potatoes before planting. This ensures an earlier, heavier crop and that only viable tubers are planted. Stand the tubers in a shallow box fitted with pillars at the corners 7.5 cm (3 in) higher than the sides.

6   In January (earlies), February (maincrop), set the tubers with the eye end uppermost — that is the end with most eyes (arrow).

7   The corner pillars allow one box to be stacked upon another. Sufficient air and light enter the gap.

8 Keep the sprouting tubers as near to 8° C (46° F) as possible, certainly free of frost. Avoid high humidity. Your larder may be just right.

9 The aim is to produce dark-coloured, short, sturdy shoots, as here.

10 Spindly, white sprouts result from too warm and too dark conditions.

11 Rub these off and start again, or cut back to the first joint.

12 Where space is limited you can sprout seed potatoes by threading them on string with a darning needle and hanging in suitable conditions.

13 Watch for greenfly on the sprouts and be ready to spray with insecticide.

14 Maincrop tubers may produce more sprouts than are needed. Quite early rub the weaker off with your thumb, leaving the two or three best.

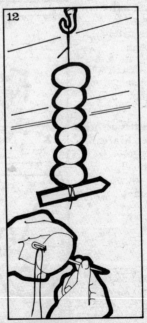

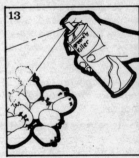

104

15 You can economise by cutting the better endowed tubers into pieces each with at least one good shoot. Plant immediately after.

16 Take out flat-bottomed drills 10 cm (4 in) deep on light soil, 15 cm (6 in) on heavy. Rows should be 60 cm (24 in) apart for earlies and second-earlies, 76 cm (30 in) for maincrops.

17 Sprinkle a little moist peat or leafmould down the bottom of the drill.

18 Set the tubers eye end uppermost, earlies 30 cm (12 in) apart, second-earlies and maincrops 38 cm (15 in).

19 Mark the ends of the rows.

20 Fill the drills by drawing soil into them with a hoe.

21 Finally, lightly fork between the rows to remove footprints.

22 If growth appears when frost threatens, give temporary protection by drawing a little soil over them.

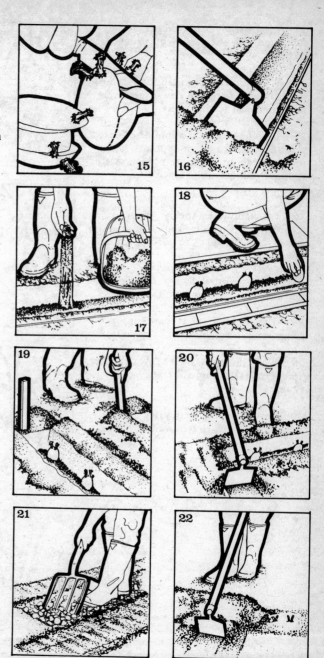

23   Alternatively, early shoots can be protected with a scattering of garden compost.

24   When growth is too tall for compost protection, put tents of newspaper over the plants, just for the night.

25   If no fertiliser was applied before planting, or if growth disappoints, when shoots are about 10 cm (4 in) high scatter fertiliser round the plants without touching the leaves.

26   Preferably use a special potato fertiliser or the mixture shown here at the rate of 105 g per m (3 oz per yd) run of row.

27   When growth is 15 cm (6 in) high hoe between the rows to kill weeds.

28   Then draw about 10 cm (4 in) of soil around the plants.

29   When the plants have grown another 15 cm (6 in) draw up a further 5 cm (2 in).

30   Earthing completed, prick lightly between the rows to remove footmarks.

31 With earlies there is no more to do until lifting, but maincrops must be sprayed with copper fungicide to ward off the ubiquitous potato blight disease.

32 Spray below the leaves as well as on top, late June in SW England, early July in Wales and other parts of England except the NE and there and in Scotland, in mid-July. Repeat fornightly.

33 Earlies should be ready in June. When they have flowered, delve into the side of the ridge with your finger: if large enough tubers are found, lift.

34 Maincrop potatoes are ready when the top growth (haulm) starts to die.

35 "Clear the decks" by cutting off the haulm with shears and burning it.

36 Insert the digging fork at the side of the ridge well away from the stems.

37 Press the fork well under the plant, lever up and twist.

38 Potatoes for storing should be left on the soil surface for a few hours to dry.

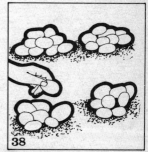

39 By growing potatoes under black polythene, you avoid earthing up and ease the work of harvesting. Unroll a strip of plastic down the row.

40 Cover the edges and ends with soil to anchor them.

41 For each tuber to be planted, cut a cross with a razor blade and plant through the slits. With each tuber put a few anti-slug pellets.

42 As the potatoes grow, guide the shoots through the holes in the plastic.

43 At harvest time, cut the haulm and lift the plastic. There are the potatoes, ready to be taken.

44 Extra-early potatoes can be grown in a heated greenhouse with a temperature of 7 to 10°C (45 to 50°F). Half-fill large pots with rich potting compost.

45 Set one or two early, sprouting tubers in each pot and cover with 7 cm (3 in) more of compost.

46 As the potatoes grow, earth up to the rim. After 10 weeks turn out a plant to see if the crop is ready.

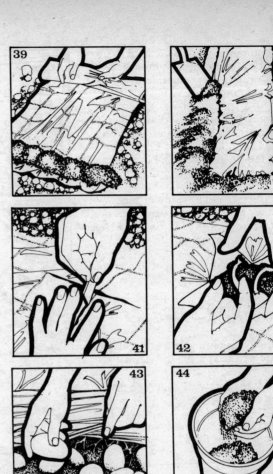

potatoes — recommended varieties

Early

Foremost. Oval. White skin. White flesh. Very early, good for forcing. Good cooking quality.

Pentland Javelin. Oval. White skin. White flesh. Good for making chips. Slightly earlier and heavier cropper than Arran Pilot. Resistant to potato eelworm.

Pentland Lustre. Pear-shaped. Skin partly pink. Firm, pale cream flesh. Resistant to potato eelworm.

Arran Pilot. Kidney-shaped. White skin. White flesh. Long a favourite for its high yield. Not of highest quality.

Home Guard. Oval. White skin. White flesh. Another old favourite for yield. Good for exhibition. Rather soft when cooked.

Epicure. Round. White skin. White flesh. Superb flavour. Rather deep eyes. Susceptible to wart disease and must never be grown on infected land.

Second-early

Maris Peer. Round. White skin. Creamy-white flesh. Heavy cropper.

Maincrop

Pentland Dell. Kidney-shaped. White skin. White flesh which cooks firm but slightly mealy. Yields as heavily as Majestic. Keeps well. Resists blight disease.

Pentland Crown. Oval. White skin. White flesh. Heavy cropper. Shallow eyes. Cooks well.

Desiree. Long oval-kidney. Skin partly pink. Pale lemon flesh. Slightly earlier than Majestic with comparable yield. Mild flavour. Moderately soft and mealy after cooking.

Majestic. Oval-kidney. White skin. White flesh. Cooks and keeps well. Suited most soils and has been popular for its heavy yield.

King Edward. Kidney-shaped. Pink skin. Long a favourite for its cooking quality. Not a very heavy yielder. Requires medium to heavy soil. Susceptible to wart disease and must never be grown on infected land.

Salad potatoes

Pink Fir Apple. Long, rather irregular shape. Pink skin. Pale lemon flesh. Waxy texture, ideal for salads and for frying. Not a heavy cropper.

other root crops

The true root crops should never be grown on freshly dunged ground as this causes the roots to fork. However this does not mean that they will succeed in poor soil. The usual practice is to grow them on deeply dug ground which was manured for the previous crop. But if fertility is in doubt a mild dressing of fertiliser is scattered prior to sowing.

1   Beetroots may be long (A), round (B), or intermediate or cylindrical (C). Usually they are red but a golden beet (D) is now available. They all taste alike. Sowings of a round type from late March to mid-April will give roots for summer salads. Sow the maincrop (for storing) from mid-May to early June.

2   You can sow beet thinly in 2.5 cm (1 in) deep drills, rows 30 cm (1 ft) apart.

3   Or, as each "seed" is really a capsule containing several seeds you can avoid unnecessary thinning by sowing clusters of two or three at 10 cm (4 in) intervals for round and cylindrical varieties, 15 cm (6 in) for long.

4   As seedlings grow thin those in continuous rows to 10 cm (4 in) apart (round and cylindrical kinds) or 15 cm (6 in) for long.

5   Thin those in clusters to the strongest in each group.

6   When hoeing beet draw a little soil up to the roots to prevent their tops becoming exposed.

7   Pull up round beet for salads while still quite small.

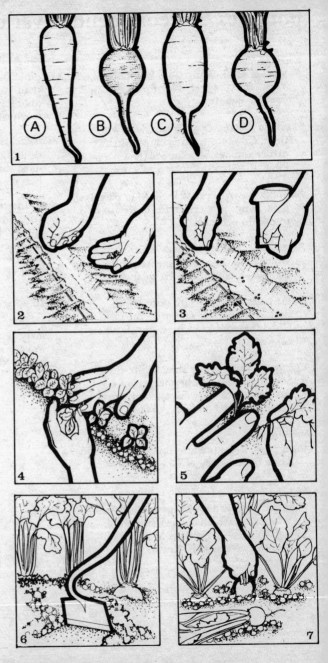

8 Beetroots should never be left too long or they become coarse and crack.

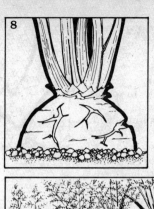

9 Lift round varieties for storage when cricket ball size, and long and cylindrical kinds in September.

10 Carrots can vary in size and shape from the small, very stumpy ones, almost round (A) which are popular for the first sowings, through various sizes of stump-rooted types (B) to the pointed ones which may be of medium length (C) or quite long (D), the latter being suitable for winter storage.

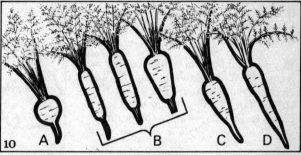

11 Sow carrots from March to July in 2 cm (¾ in) deep drills, 23 cm (9 in) apart for stump-rooted kinds 30 cm (12 in) for pointed. Use the rake to cover the seeds.

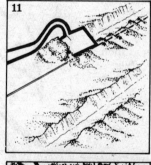

12 Thin gradually several times, until small roots are 5 cm (2 in) apart, large-rooted kinds 10 cm (4 in), always pressing the soil firmly back round those remaining.

13 Don't let the tops of the carrots become exposed as this greens them. Lift as required for use, storing roots in October.

14 Raise seedlings of celeriac, which has root-like swollen stems, celery-flavoured, like celery and plant out in well-manured soil in June, 30 cm (12 in) apart, rows 45 cm (18 in) apart. Lift for use as required.

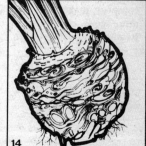

15   Unlike beetroots and carrots, scrape soil away from celeriac roots to help them swell.

16   Chinese artichokes are an uncommon tuberous vegetable. In spring plant 23 cm (9 in) apart, rows 46 cm (18 in) apart. Lift for use in autumn and winter.

17   Plant Jerusalem artichokes as early in the year as the soil will permit, 38 cm (15 in) apart, rows 90 cm (3 ft) apart. Lift the tubers in autumn and winter as required.

18   Sow kohl rabi in well manured ground from spring to mid-July, rows 38 cm (15 in) apart. Thin to 25 cm (10 in). Cook bulbous stems while still young and tender, or store for autumn use.

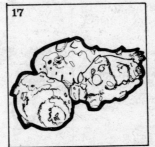

19   Parsnips are a very hardy root. Choose a short kind (left) for shallow soils.

20   Sow parsnips in March, or as soon after as the soil is workable, in drills 30 cm (12 in) apart.

21   For long parsnips, make 75 cm (2½ ft) deep holes with an iron bar at 20 cm (8 in) intervals.

22   Fill these holes with potting compost, make firm, wait a week and sow three seeds, later thinning to the one strongest, at each station.

23   Where parsnips have been sown in a drill, thin in easy stages until the remaining seedlings are 15 cm (6 in) apart.

24   Lift parsnips in late October or November for storage or leave until required for use. For long roots dig a trench alongside the roots to facilitate lifting.

25   Salsify roots have a delicate oyster-like flavour. Sow in spring, drills 38 cm (15 in) apart and thin to 23 cm (9 in) apart. Lift in late autumn for use as required.

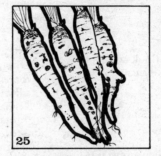

26   Scorzonera, much like salsify but with a stronger flavour. Sow in early May, as for salsify, and start lifting in early October. Cook whole without scraping.

27   Swedes (left) and turnips are much alike. In summer use turnips while still small and young. Both may be lifted in late autumn for storage or left in the ground for use as required.

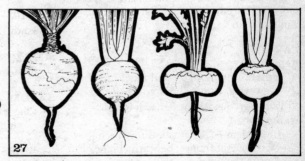

28   Sow the first turnips in early April, with succession sowings until early July. Sow swedes in mid-June, turnips for storage late in July. Make drills 2 cm (¾ in) deep, 38 cm (15 in) apart. Thin turnips to 15 cm (6 in) apart, swedes to 30 cm (1 ft).

29   Use a fork to lever up root vegetables without damage to them. Always lift and store some in case frozen soil prevents lifting for periods in mid-winter.

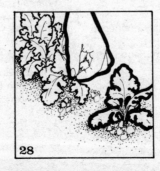

other root crops — recommended varieties

BEETROOT
Round:
    Early Bunch. Best for very early sowing.
    Boltardy. Can be sown very early, and
      late, without risk of running to seed.
      A very reliable variety of quality.
    Crimson Globe. Very dark red.
Long:
    Cheltenham Green Top.
Cylindrical:
    Housewives' Choice.
Yellow:
    Golden. Does not bleed. Cook and
      serve hot or cold like normal
      beetroot.
White:
    Snowhite. Does not bleed. Suitable
      for serving with fish.

The foliage of both the Golden and
Snowhite varieties may also be cooked
and served like spinach.

CARROTS
Round:
    Parisian Rondo. Early and quick
      growing. Roots about golf ball size.
    Paris Forcing. As for Parisian Rondo.
Stump-rooted:
    Amsterdam Forcing. Good for forcing,
      growing in frames, beneath cloches
      or in the open.
    Nantes Express.
    Chantenay Red Cored. Early maincrop.
Pointed:
    James' Scarlet Intermediate. Good
      variety for storing.
    St. Valery. Good variety for storing.

CELERIAC
    Marble Ball.
    Globus.
    Iram.

CHINESE ARTICHOKE
    No varieties.

JERUSALEM ARTICHOKE
    Fuseau.
    Silver Skinned.

KOHL RABI
    White Vienna.
    Purple Vienna.

PARSNIPS
Short-rooted:
    Avonresister. Resists parsnip canker
      disease.
    Offenham.
Long-rooted:
    Improved Hollow Crown.
    Tender and True. For the longest roots.

SALSIFY
    Sandwich Island.

SCORZONERA
    Russian Giant.

SWEDES
    Chignecto. Purple-topped. Resists
      club root disease.

TURNIPS
Flat-rooted:
    White Milan. Early.
    Purple Milan. Early
Round:
    Snowball. Early. Good for first
      sowings and summer use.
    Golden Ball. Hardy. Good for
      storing.

the pod-bearers

The pod bearing vegetables (the legumes) include some of the most popular of all kitchen garden crops. Broad beans are one of the easiest to grow, green peas somewhat more difficult. All do best on well-manured, deeply cultivated and only slightly acid soil and require an abundance of water during the growing season.

1   In the warmest, most favoured districts only, the earliest broad beans may be secured by sowing a variety of the longpod group (the hardiest) in late October.

2   When cloches are available you can have an early picking by sowing in January or early February (no earlier) and keeping covered until late March or early April.

3   In most gardens it is safer for the first outdoor sowing to wait until the soil can be broken down to a fine tilth in February or March.

4   Take out a flat-bottomed drill 7.5 cm (3 in) deep and 25 cm (10 in) wide.

5   Space the seeds 23 cm (9 in) apart in two rows 23 cm (9 in) apart, staggering the seed in the rows.

6   Plant a few extra seeds to provide replacements for any gaps. Allow 60 cm (2 ft) between rows.

7   For an extra-early crop you can also sow seeds in February, 5 cm (2 in) apart, 2 cm (¾ in) deep, in a deep box.

8   Start them in the greenhouse, max. temperature 15°C (60°F), harden in a cold frame and plant outdoors in April.

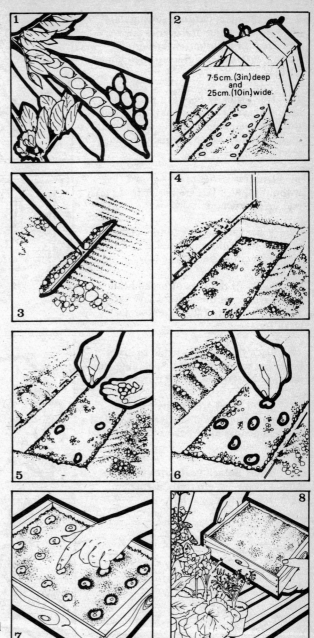

9   For the main outdoor sowing (late March-April) Windsor varieties are preferred for their better flavour and home freezers prefer green-seeded kinds (right).

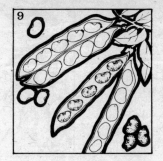

10   Hoe regularly between the broad bean plants and remove basal sideshoots from the maincrop kinds, but don't thin dwarf varieties which normally produce several stems.

11   Dwarf varieties can be grown without support but are better for at least one string down each side of the row.

12   Taller varieties need more elaborate support with substantial stakes and two strings on either side of the row.

13   Pinch off the tops of broad bean plants as soon as the flowers have set. This helps pods to fill and discourages black fly.

14   Black fly is always liable to infest broad beans. Forestall it by spraying with systemic insecticide before flowers open.

15   Broad beans are usually podded before cooking but are delicious if picked while immature and cooked whole, served in white sauce.

16   Dwarf French beans are similar to runner beans but are ready earlier and with their own special flavour.

17 Most dwarf French bean varieties today are stringless and remain so even when the seeds within are fairly well developed and make prominent bulges down the pod.

18 In early May sow French beans 11 cm (4½ in) apart in single drills 5 cm (2 in) deep, rows 45 cm (18 in) apart. Make successional sowings at 3-week intervals until mid-July.

19 Where cloches are available set them in place early in March, to warm the soil, and sow at the end of the month.

20 Dwarf beans do not need individual stakes but a string on either side of the row will keep lower trusses off the ground.

21 Grow climbing French beans in the same way as the dwarf but set rows 90 cm (3 ft) apart and provide a support for each.

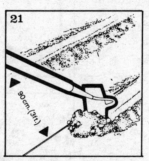

22 Runner beans are easy to grow. They repay being given a rich site with immense crops.

23 If the plot was not manured, take out a spade-deep trench for the runners in winter and work manure into the bottom.

24 Replace the top soil and leave to settle before breaking down finely ready for sowing in May.

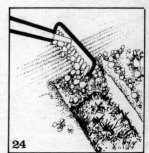

117

25   Runner beans are very vulnerable to frost but you can steal a march by sowing seeds singly in small pots in mid-April, starting them indoors or in the greenhouse.

26   Harden off the runner bean seedlings in a cold frame but always be ready to give extra night protection when frost threatens.

27   Plant these early seedlings in late May. Give "local protection" by folding a length of polythene over a string.

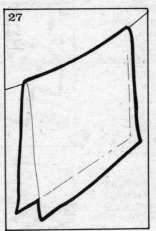

28   Tie this polythene round the bean sticks and plant the beans in between.

29   Sow runner beans in the open 5 cm (2 in) deep and 23 cm (9 in) apart in double rows 30 cm (12 in) apart.

30   Systems of support for runner beans are legion. Remember that in full growth they are heavy and present a formidable barrier to the wind. If blown down the crop comes to a premature end.

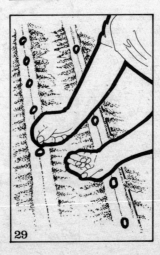

31   The most popular way to support runner beans is with hazel bean poles, one per plant, with a horizontal pole at the apex to give stability.

32   If space permits cross the poles low down, then most of the beans will hang on the outer side, more accessible for picking.

33   Bamboo canes may be used instead of poles (cheaper, too, if you grow your own) but stouter posts will be needed at intervals and along the ridge.

34   Canes may also be erected wigwam fashion, setting them in fours and tying at the top.

35   Strings or wide-mesh netting may be used provided there are strong upright poles at intervals and along the top. Tie vertical strings to a horizontal string at the bottom.

36   To avoid tangling in the early stages of growth, help the runners to find their appointed supports. Gently twist them round, remembering that they only twist anti-clockwise.

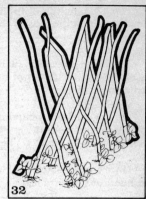

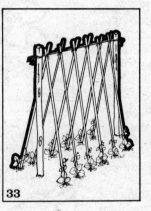

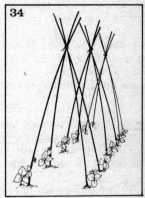

37 Pinch off the tips of runner beans when they reach the tops of their supports.

38 Where poles are unavailable, grow one of the dwarf varieties of runner needing no staking.

39 Or you can keep a climbing runner short by pinching out the growing point when less than 30 cm (1 ft) high.

40 Once a week pinch out the resultant sideshoots at the third leaf.

41 With all runner beans it is most important to pick frequently. Once seeds begin to form further growth slows down.

42 When cloches are available the first pea sowing, for May picking (a dwarf, round-seeded variety) can be in October (in the north), November (in the south).

43 You can make a second cloche sowing in early February, but the first unprotected sowing should not be made until late February or early March — and then only if the soil will rake down well.

44 For peas take out flat-bottomed drills 5 cm (2 in) deep and about 20 cm (8 in) wide, using the spade and keeping the blade almost horizontal.

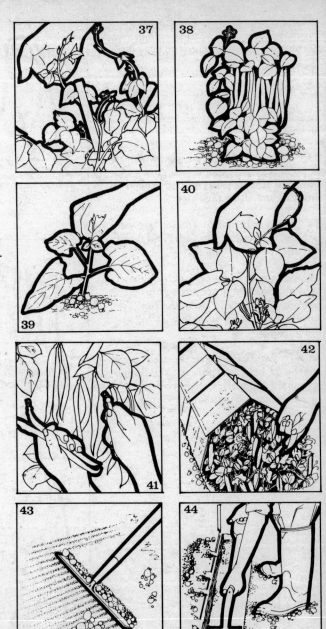

45 Space out pea seeds 7.5 cm (3 in) apart in three rows, 7.5 cm (3 in) apart. Further sowings may be made until early July.

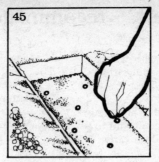

46 For later sowings sow in a deeper drill and only half fill it to cover the seed. This depression will hold the moisture when you water.

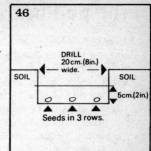

47 For winter cloche sowings and where mice are notably troublesome scatter bits of gorse before covering the seed.

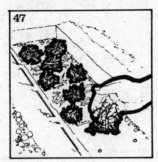

48 Or, before sowing peas, shake the seeds in a can with a little paraffin and then roll them in red lead.

49 The space between pea rows should be equal to their expected height or, if different, the mean of the two.

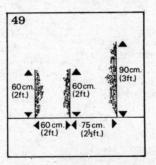

50 When the seedlings are about 10 cm (4 in) high hoe between them and insert pieces of twiggy brushwood to give early support.

51 In the early stages a strip of wire netting will protect from birds. Later it may be necessary to net over the rows.

52 All varieties growing 60 cm (2 ft) or higher will need support — either twiggy peasticks or netting.

the pod-bearers — recommended varieties

BROAD BEANS
Longpod varieties (hardiest, for winter, cloche and earliest spring sowings)
    Aquadulce. White seeds. Best for autumn sowing.
    Imperial White Longpod. White seeds. Very large pods containing up to 9 beans. Recommended for early spring sowing.
    Imperial Green Longpod. Green seeds. As for Imperial White Longpod.
Dwarf
    The Sutton. White seeds. Suitable for cloche and later sowing in open. Grows 30 cm (1 ft) high.
Windsor varieties.
    Imperial White Windsor. White seeds. For later spring sowings. Up to 7 or 8 beans per pod.
    Imperial Green Windsor. Green seeds. As for Imperial White Windsor.

FRENCH BEANS
Dwarf
    The Prince. Old favourite. Very early. Good for cloches. Almost stringless if picked young.
    Flair. Round-oval pods. Early. Stringless.
    Kinghorn Waxpod. Fleshy pods. Stringless.
    Glamis. Stringless. Specially recommended for Scottish and northern gardens.
    Granda. May be eaten green or seeds dried for winter use.
Climbing
    Earliest of All. Good cropper. Seeds may be dried as haricots.

RUNNER BEANS
Climbing
    Enorma. Heavy cropper of long, slender pods. Good for deep freezing.
    Sunset. Quick maturing. Medium length pods.
    Fry. Stringless. White-seeded.

Dwarf
    Hammonds Dwarf Scarlet. Red flowers. Pods 20—23 cm (8—9 in) long, grows 40 cm (16 in) high.
    Hammonds Dwarf White. As the Scarlet but with white flowers and white seeds.

PEAS
(The heights given below are approximate)
Round-seeded (hardiest, usually quicker growing)
    Feltham First. 45 cm (1½ ft). Suitable for cloche sowing and very early sowing in the open.
    Meteor. 45 cm (1½ ft). Suitable for cloche sowing and very early sowing in the open.
    The Pilot. 1 m (3½ ft). Heavy cropper. Good for early sowing in the open.

Wrinkle-seeded (sweeter flavoured)
EARLY (maturing in about 10 weeks)
    Sweetness. 90 cm (3 ft). Very early.
    Kelvedon Wonder. 45 cm (1½ ft). Good for cloches and in the open.
    (Sow early varieties late for the last crops of the season)

SECOND-EARLY (maturing in about 12—13 weeks)
    Early Onward. 60 cm (2 ft). Good flavour.

MAINCROP (maturing in about 14—15 weeks)
    Onward. 75 cm (2½ ft). Very widely grown.
    Achievement. 1.2 to 1.5 m (4—5 ft). Very long pods.
    Lord Chancellor. 0.9 to 1.2 m (3—4 ft). Late. Very heavy cropper.

the onion family

The most prominent members of this health-giving family are the ordinary onion itself and the leek. Others include shallots, garlic and chives. Onions have rather particular soil needs and as they will grow well in the same plot year after year, many gardeners follow this practice so that gradually the soil may be brought nearer the rich, deeply-worked, friable consistency which is the ideal. Onions will not thrive on poorly drained, very heavy or extremely light soil, preferring one on the light side of medium. Work in manure liberally the autumn before growing an onion crop.

1 Onions may be flattish (A), globular (B) or top-shaped like an elongated globe (C). Shape, however, is relatively unimportant. What is vital is to choose a variety appropriate to the method of culture to be followed.

2 For large bulbs start early, sowing outdoors in late August (in the south), early in the month (in the north). Rake the seedbed to a fine tilth.

3 Sow not too thinly in drills 2 cm (¾ in) deep and 30 cm (1 ft) apart. Leave the seedlings unthinned through the winter.

4 In early March lift the seedlings with a handfork.

5 Transplant to the onion bed, 17 cm (7 in) apart in rows 30 cm (1 ft) apart.

6 More reliable results follow sowing under glass. Sow thinly in pots or boxes of sowing compost.

7 Preferably start in the greenhouse, 10–16° C (50–60° F) in January.

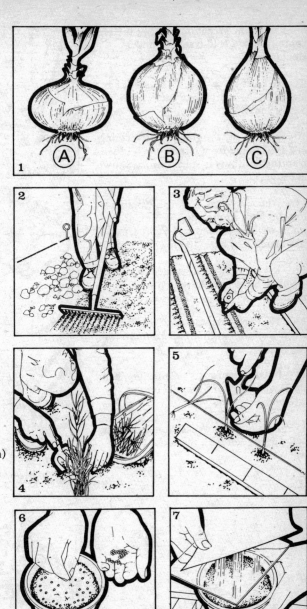

8 Failing the greenhouse, stand the seed containers in a cold frame or under cloches.

9 Prick off these under-glass seedlings 4 cm (1½ in) apart when they are about 5 cm (2 in) high.

10 Harden off the greenhouse seedlings in a cold frame from late March on for planting outdoors in mid-April, as shown in frame 5.

11 Where no glass is available onions may be sown in the open as soon as the soil is friable between mid-February and late March. Set rows 30 cm (1 ft) apart.

12 Keep onions well weeded. When seedlings are 5 cm (2 in) high start thinning. Use later thinnings for salads.

13 Thin progressively until the onions are at least 15 cm (6 in) apart, more for large bulbs.

14 In late August, to aid ripening, bend the leaves over until they lie on the ground.

15 Two or three weeks later loosen the bulbs in the soil with the fork.

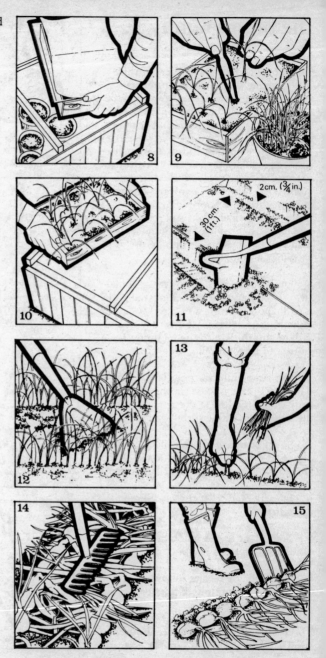

16 In late September lift completely. In drought conditions they can dry on the bed. August-sown bulbs will be ready by late July or early August, glass-raised bulbs by early September.

17 If the soil is damp, spread the bulbs on a dry surface until the tops have withered. Be ready to protect or take under cover if rain threatens.

18 Where onion growing has been found difficult try buying sets. These are dried immature bulbs which later make bulbs of fair size.

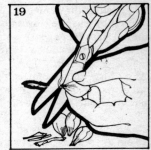

19 Before planting onion sets cut off the whiskery remains of old leaves which attract the curiosity of birds.

20 Plant onion sets in March so that their tips are just exposed.

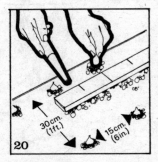

21 Look the sets over frequently in early weeks to replace bulbs dislodged by birds.

22 Should flower stems appear, pinch these off at once.

23 Special onions for salads may be grown by sowing in drills 23 cm (9 in) apart in mid-August and from March to June.

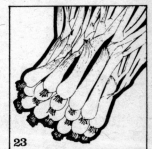

24   Plant shallots in late February or early March, as with onion sets, with their tips showing.

25   As shallots grow, scrape a little soil from around the bulbs to help them swell into clusters.

26   When shallot foliage turns yellow in late July, lift the clumps and dry in the sun.

27   Plant garlic in March, splitting the bulbs into separate cloves and setting these 15 cm (6 in) apart in drills 5 cm (2 in) deep, rows 30 cm (1 ft) apart.

28   Chives are perennials, their leaves cut as required to impart a very mild onion flavour. Don't let them flower

29   Sow chives in spring or plant clumps 30 cm (1 ft) apart. When clumps become overcrowded, lift; divide into clusters of about six and replant.

30   Leeks like a deep rich soil but are less particular than onions. Being quite hardy you can leave them in the ground until required for use during the winter.

31   For extra large exhibition quality stems sow in the greenhouse in January or February and harden off in a cold frame to plant outdoors in May.

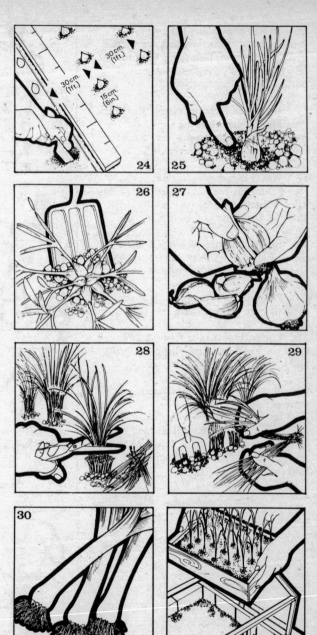

32   For normal kitchen use sow leeks in an outdoor seedbed from early March to mid-April. Make shallow drills 30 cm (1 ft) apart.

33   Thin the leek seedlings early and during June and July transplant in batches to provide a succession.

34   Water the seedbed the night before lifting. Trim the tips of the leaves with scissors.

35   The quick way to plant leeks is with a trowel in 15 cm (6 in) deep drills. Let the drills fill gradually as the leeks grow.

36   But a better method is to make holes about 25 cm (10 in) deep with a dibber, 23 cm (9 in) apart, rows 38 cm (15 in) apart.

37   Drop one leek in each hole. Don't fill with soil but water in.

38   With successive waterings the hole round the leek plant will gradually fill.

39   Later, to increase the length of blanched stem, draw up soil round the plants whether planted in drills or holes.

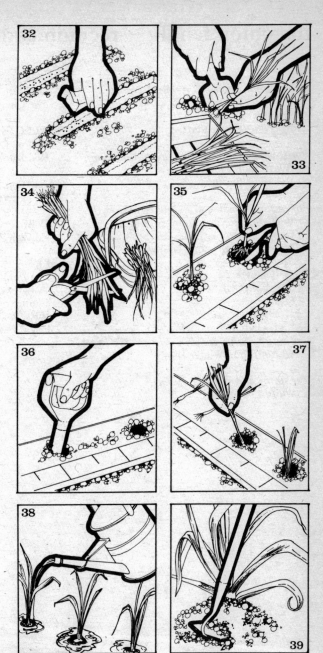

the onion family — recommended varieties

ONIONS
For outdoor sowing in August:
  Reliance. Flattish.
  Solidity. Flattish.
  Express Yellow. Flattish.

For sowing in warmth in January/February:
  Ailsa Craig. Globular.
  Reliance. Flattish.

For outdoor sowing in February/March:
  Bedfordshire Champion. Globular.
  Giant Zittau. Flattish.
  James Long Keeping. Globular.

ONION SETS
  Stuttgarter Giant
  Sturon

SALAD ONIONS
For autumn sowing only:
  White Lisbon Winter Hardy

For spring and summer sowing:
  White Lisbon

PICKLING ONIONS
  Cocktail
  The Queen

SHALLOTS
  Yellow Dutch
  Red Dutch

GARLIC
  No varieties.

CHIVES
  No varieties.

LEEKS
  The Lyon (also called Prizetaker).
    Early. Recommended for sowing
    under glass.
  Musselburgh. Maincrop.
  Royal Favourite.

cucumbers

Cucumbers are of two types, greenhouse or frame and ridge or outdoor. The latter used to be despised because of their inferior size but of recent years they have been greatly improved. They are of equal eating quality to the greenhouse varieties — although still shorter than the others — and this makes the ridge cucumber more convenient for many households. With artificial heating, greenhouse cucumbers are available over a much longer season than the outdoor. Cucumbers often have to share a greenhouse with tomatoes but this is undesirable because they thrive in higher temperatures and a much moister atmosphere than tomatoes will readily tolerate.

1   Typical greenhouse cucumbers.

2   Ridge cucumbers. A small-fruited kind (gherkin) may be grown for pickling.

3   For the earliest outdoor (ridge) cucumbers sow in small pots in the latter half of April. Sow two seeds, on edge, in each, about 2.5 cm (1 in) deep.

4   Cover with glass and a sheet of newspaper and place in the greenhouse, temperature 18° C (65° F).

5   As soon as growth is visible, remove the covers.

6   When the seedlings are well up, pinch out the weaker of each pair.

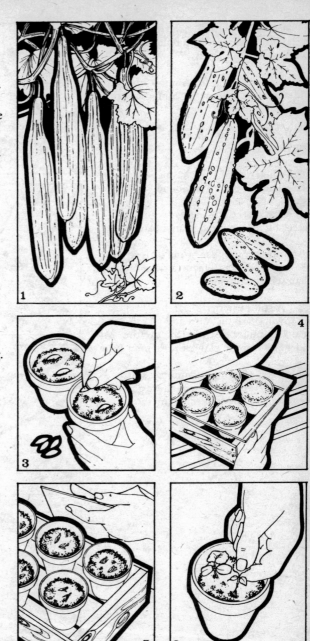

7   Meanwhile prepare rich sites outdoors by taking out spade-deep holes at 90 cm (3 ft) intervals.

8   Fork in manure or compost liberally and mix more manure or compost with the excavated soil.

9   Replace the soil in the hole to make a low mound.

10   When risk of frost has passed, plant one cucumber on each mound.

11   For a later crop, sow two seeds direct on each mound in mid-May.

12   Where a number of plants is to be grown it is easier to make a ridge rather than separate mounds.

13   A still earlier crop can be obtained by sowing early in April and planting in mid-May under cloches. Remove the cloches when the plants fill them in June.

14   After planting cucumbers, scatter slug pellets round them as these pests are very fond of the tender young shoots.

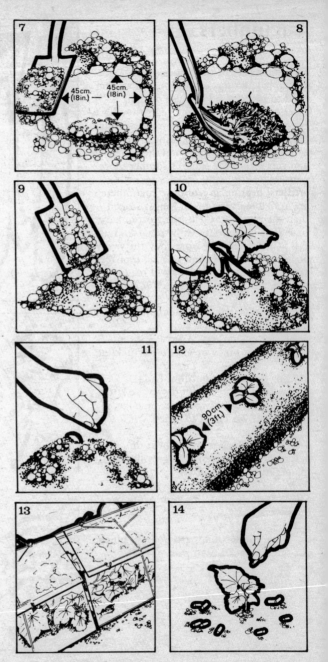

15   To induce branching, pinch out the growing points of ridge cucumbers when 6—8 leaves have been made.

16   Ridge cucumbers only develop when female flowers are pollinated by male flowers, so never remove the latter.

17   Start greenhouse cucumbers like the ridge, sowing two seeds per small pot. Begin in January or early February, provided a minimum night temperature of 18°C (65°C) can be maintained. For this a heated propagator within the greenhouse is useful.

18   Pinch out the smaller of each pair of seedlings and when four rough leaves have appeared transfer to a larger pot, about 13 cm (5 in) size.

19   When 6—8 rough leaves have been made transplant to large pots 25 cm (10 in) or larger, using a mixture of half strawy but well-rotted manure with half loam, or John Innes potting compost No. 3.

20   Or make up a bed on the greenhouse staging, using planks or a large box to hold the soil in.

21   But best of all is to plant in a bed of the rich soil mixture or potting compost made on the floor of the house. Set each plant on a slight mound or along a ridge.

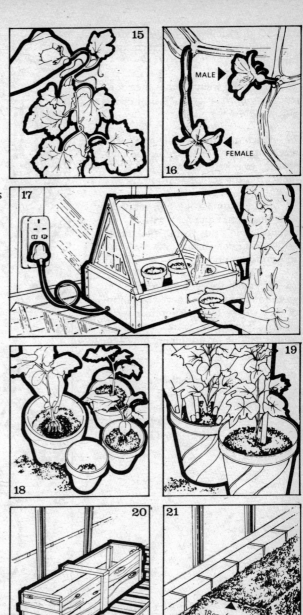

22   Set the cucumber plants at 90 cm (3 ft) intervals and provide each with a cane support.

23   When the stem reaches the roof, train it to horizontal wires about 33 cm (13 in) below the glass.

24   Pinch out the growing point when it reaches the apex of the roof. Tie side growths to horizontal wires and stop them after the second leaf joint.

25   Shade from strong sun, spray daily with clear water and feed with liquid manure when fruits form. When roots show on the soil surface, cover with additional compost.

26   Unlike ridge cucumbers the greenhouse type must never be pollinated or they will be bitter. Therefore remove all male flowers. Some new varieties save us this trouble by producing only female flowers.

27   For growing in cold frames sow late March/early April and plant in early May, one per frame light. Pinch when six leaves have been made and train four side shoots to the corners of the frame, then stop.

cucumbers — recommended varieties

RIDGE (OUTDOOR CUCUMBERS)

Baton Vert. Long fruits. Quick maturing. Excellent flavour.

Burpee Hybrid. Large fruits. Remarkably prolific.

Burpless. Bred in Japan, there are several Burpless varieties which are less bitter and more easily digested than ordinary cucumbers. Tasty Green has long, thin dark green fruits and is prolific. Green King produces mostly female fruits and Burpless Early is very quick maturing.

GHERKINS

Venlo Pickling. Very prolific.

Conda. Very prolific. Early.

GREENHOUSE OR FRAME CUCUMBERS

Butcher's Disease Resisting. Resists some diseases. Medium size fruits. Heavy cropper. Suitable for greenhouse or frame culture.

Conqueror. A reliable general-purpose variety. Popular for unheated houses and frames. Specially suitable where cucumbers are to be grown in a house with tomatoes.

Telegraph Improved. An improved form of an old exhibitor's favourite. Does well in heated or unheated houses and in frames.

Femspot. Produces all female flowers. Very early but fruits over long season. Resists some diseases.

Rocket. Produces all female flowers. Very heavy cropper. Recommended for greenhouse culture. Resists some diseases.

tomatoes

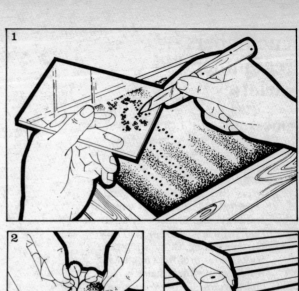

You can grow tomatoes in the open or under glass. The outdoor season is short and heaviest crops are produced in greenhouses. Outdoors the best chances of success are in southern and warm districts and, of course, in good summers. Both outdoor and greenhouse plants must be raised under glass. To grow very early or very late greenhouse tomatoes requires considerable skill and heat, and is best only attempted with experience. For an early greenhouse crop sow in January but the beginner should wait until late February. A temperature of 16 to 18°C (60—65° F) is necessary.

1   Sow tomatoes in either John Innes or a soilless compost, spacing the seeds 2.5 cm (1 in) apart each way. Spread the seeds on a sheet of glass and flick them off singly with a pencil point or penknife. Sieve .3 cm ($\frac{1}{8}$ in) of compost over the seeds, moisten with a fine rose on the can and cover with glass and newspaper until germination.

2   As soon as seedlings can be handled, transfer to small pots. Hold them by their seed (first) leaves, never by the stem.

3   Temperature at this stage should be from 10 to 16°C (50—60° F). After three weeks turn out a sample pot. If roots are visible move into the 10 cm (4 in) size.

4   When roots fill the second pots, transfer the plants to final quarters. These may be large pots, at least 23 cm (9 in) size, or boxes.

5   Or you can fruit tomatoes in troughs on the greenhouse staging. For final quarters use John Innes potting compost or a good fibrous soil.

6 Another possibility is to plant in polythene bags of soilless compost which are sold for this purpose.

7 Where the soil has not been infected by previous tomato troubles you can plant direct in a greenhouse border.

8 Provide each plant with a cane support. Tie the stem to this loosely but securely with soft string or raffia.

9 Keep each plant to a single stem removing any sideshoots as soon as they appear in leaf joints with the point of a penknife.

10 When flowers open, spray with clear water around noon to aid fruit-setting. Ventilate freely when temperature exceeds 16° C (60° F).

11 A gradually increasing amount of water will be required. When fruits swell begin feeding with a proprietary liquid tomato manure.

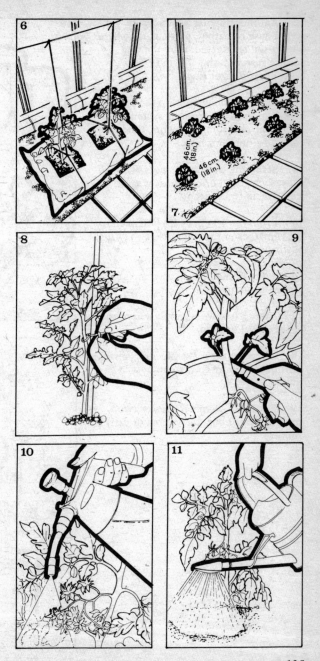

12 Another popular way to grow greenhouse tomatoes, particularly where border soil is infected, is by the ring culture system, using 23 cm (9 in) bottomless pots or rings.

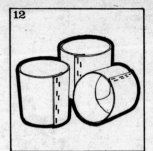

13 The system depends on the plant's ability to form two rooting systems, the upper one absorbing nutrients, the lower collecting only moisture.

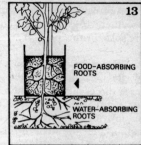

14 Stand the bottomless pots on a bed of washed gravel or coarse river sand, at least 16 cm (6 in) deep.

15 From the 10 cm (4 in) pots plant the tomatoes in the rings, using the usual potting compost.

16 Stake in the normal way and at first water the compost in the rings.

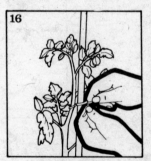

17 After a few weeks apply water only to the gravel or sand.

18 When fruits set start feeding, giving the liquid manure to the compost in the ring.

19 For outdoor tomatoes sow two seeds per small pot, late March or early April.

20 Pinch out the weaker seedling of each pair.

21 When roots fill the seed-pots pot on to the 10 cm (4 in) size.

22 In May harden the young plants in a coldframe.

23 Plant in the open in early June, 45 cm (18 in) apart, 76 cm (30 in) between rows.

24 For cordon tomatoes stake each plant separately and remove all sideshoots promptly.

25 Pinch out the growing tip of each plant when four trusses have set.

26 In late summer untie cordon tomatoes, lay on strawed ground and cover with cloches to aid ripening of last fruits.

27 With bush varieties don't pinch sideshoots but straw the ground to keep fruit clean and scatter slug pellets.

tomatoes — recommended varieties

For heated greenhouses:

Ailsa Craig. Unsurpassed flavour and thin-skinned. But not an easy variety to grow. Liable to suffer from greenback (incomplete colouring of skin) and vulnerable to disease.

Alicante. Free from greenback. Very good eating quality and flavour.

Big Boy. Remarkable for the size of individual fruits, possibly 45 to 90 kg (1 to 2 lb) each. Restrict to 3 trusses.

Eurocross BB. Sets well in short days. Early and heavy cropping. Fruits fairly large and free of greenback. Resists leaf-mould disease.

Kirdford Cross. Resists leaf-mould and Tobacco Mosaic virus diseases. Compact habit. Good cropper of quality fruit.

Seville Cross. Resists leaf-mould. Fruits of even size, about 56 g (2 oz).

Ware Cross. Vigorous grower. Fairly large, solid fruits of good flavour.

For greenhouses unheated from April onward:

Alicante. See above.

Eurocross A. Early. Heavy cropper. Greenback free and resists leaf-mould.

Moneymaker. Easy to grow. Heavy cropper of solid, medium-sized fruit but flavour not outstanding.

Cordon varieties for planting outdoors:

Ailsa Craig. See above.

Alicante. See above.

Harbinger. Early maturing. Smallish fruit. A popular favourite.

Histon Early. Very early, heavy cropper. Fine flavour.

Moneymaker. See above.

Outdoor Girl. Very early, heavy cropper. Good quality.

Yellow varieties:

Golden Amateur. The yellow-fruited counterpart of the bush variety The Amateur, see below.

Golden Queen. Like most yellow varieties, sweeter than most red. Suitable for outdoors or under glass.

Peach. Low acid content. Fruits similar in size and shape to Moneymaker.

Yellow Perfection. Very early. Good for outdoor culture.

Bush varieties:

Sigmabush. Makes less foliage than some bush varieties. Early, yields well.

The Amateur. For long the most popular bush variety. Medium-sized fruit.

lettuce and other salads

We have dealt with cucumbers and tomatoes, beetroot and spring onions, beans, carrots and cabbage, but that by no means exhausts attractive salad possibilities. There are also celery, chicory, corn salad, dandelion, endive, radish and, king of all the salads, lettuce. Midwinter lettuce requires a heated greenhouse and considerable skill but good lettuce can be cut from the open garden from April onwards and, with the aid of cloches, almost to the end of the year. Rich soil, frequent sowings and early thinning are the secrets of success.

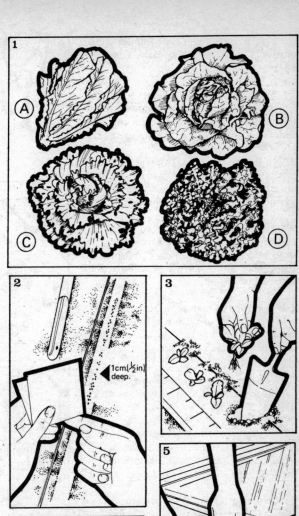

1   There are two main groups of lettuce — the tall-leaved cos (A) and the cabbage types which are themselves divided into butterheads (B), with soft, round, close-hearted heads, the crispheads (C) or crisphearts, with curly, very crisp leaves, and the looseheads (D) which do not form close hearts and have many curled leaves.

2   For the earliest outdoor lettuce without protection, sow a winter-hardy variety in late August/early September.

3   Transplant the winter seedlings in autumn, while still quite small, to 7.5 cm (3 in) apart and guard with slug pellets. In early spring thin to 23 cm (9 in) apart.

4   Where a greenhouse is available, sow lettuce in February and prick out the seedlings 7.5 cm (3 in) apart, handling only by the seedleaves.

5   In March move the seedlings to a cold frame to harden off gradually, ventilating freely in mild weather.

6   Plant the seedlings raised under glass outdoors in late March or early April, 23 cm (9 in) apart.

7   You can sow under cloches from late September (in the north) to mid-October (south and west). Make drills 15 cm (6 in) apart and thin to 7.5 cm (3 in) apart.

8   In late December transplant the cloche seedlings 30 cm (12 in) apart, still under cloches. Make more cloche sowings in mid-January and late February.

9   Make the first unprotected sowing in early March and continue fortnightly until mid-August. Thinnings, transplanted from early and late sowings, will mature a week or two later.

10   Lettuce to mature in high summer must always be sown in situ for they will not transplant. For these sowings only, a little shade is an advantage.

11   For midwinter greenhouse culture sow in September, temperature about 13° C (55° F).

12   Transplant the greenhouse lettuce close to the glass when four leaves have been made. Keep the temperature near 10° C (50° F).

13   Sow corn salad (lamb's lettuce) from March to September in drills 30 cm (12 in) apart and thin to 15 cm (6 in). Protect with cloches from November on.

14   The celery normally grown for autumn and winter use has long blanched stems. There are pink and red varieties, seldom grown, and requiring similar treatment. Celery needs rich soil, free drainage and plenty of moisture.

15   To meet these needs take out a special trench 30 cm (12 in) deep, fork manure or compost liberally into the bottom and return the soil up to 10 cm (4 in) from the top.

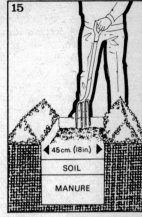

16   Meanwhile, sow seeds in the greenhouse in March, prick off the seedlings early and harden in a cold frame during May. Alternatively buy plants, as here, in late May or June.

17   Set out in two rows, water freely in dry weather and a few weeks later feed with nitrate of soda, 7.5 g per m run of row (1 oz per 12 ft), not touching the stems and raked in. Repeat the feed in a fortnight.

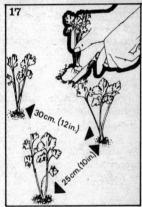

18   When the plants are 36 cm (14 in) high, cut off any sideshoots, tie the stem together with raffia and start earthing up.

19   Spread the earthing over three easy stages, at 3-week intervals, until only the tops of the leaves remain exposed.

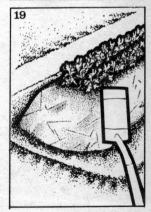

20 Where importance is attached to cleanliness of stem (as for exhibition), wrap the celery stems with corrugated cardboard or collars of brown paper before earthing.

21 In midwinter lay strips of polythene along the ridge sides to shed rain and scatter bracken over the plants to shield from frost.

22 Quick-growing self-blanching celery, and green varieties which require no blanching, should be grown for summer and early autumn use, not being so hardy. In early June plant in blocks, not rows, setting them 23 cm (9 in) apart each way. Scattering bracken or straw round the edge of the plot in early July helps to keep the outside self-blanching plants white.

23 Blanched chicory is a valuable salad early in the year. Sow in shallow drills 30 cm (12 in) apart in May and thin to 23 cm (9 in).

24 In November dig up the parsnip-like chicory roots, remove the leaves and store the roots in sand in a cool place.

25 From early December on plant chicory roots in large pots of soil. Keep moist and dark in any warm place, minimum temperature 10° C (50° F).

26 In the greenhouse you can invert one pot over the other to keep out light. In a few weeks the "chicons" will be ready to cut. Discard forced roots.

DRAINAGE HOLE FILLED TO EXCLUDE LIGHT.

27 Sugar loaf chicory is an autumn salading needing no blanching. Grow like lettuce, sowing in drills (June/July) 38 cm (15 in) apart. Thin to 25 cm (10 in).

28 Endive needs rich soil and must be blanched. The curled type has frizzy leaves. Sow April/July, drills 38 cm (15 in) apart. Thin to 30 cm (12 in).

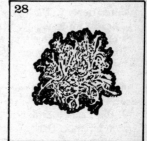

29 The broad-leaved endive is hardier and better for sowing in July/August. Cover with cloches in early October.

30 Both types of endive need blanching — by covering with pots, old dinner plates or putting black polythene over a cloche.

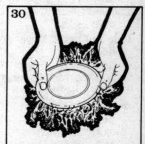

31 Sow radishes in small batches March/September. Broadcast the seed, rake in, thin early and keep well watered.

32 Winter radishes form large roots. Leave in the ground until required, then shred in salads. Sow (July) in drills 30 cm (12 in) apart. Thin to 20 cm (8 in).

143

lettuce and other salads — recommended varieties

LETTUCE
For growing outdoors in summer:
COS TYPES
    Balloon. Large headed.
    Little Gem. Medium size. Intermediate between cabbage and cos. Very sweet and crisp.
    Lobjoits Green. Large heads. Deep green.
    Winter Density. Dark green, solid heads. Intermediate between cabbage and cos. May be sown in spring and summer, also recommended for autumn sowing.

CABBAGE TYPES
Butterheads:
    All the Year Round. Solid hearted.
    Avondefiance. Dark green. Mildew-resistant. Specially recommended for July/August sowing.
    Cobham Green. Large, dark green solid heads.
    Constant Heart. Bright green, large, firm hearts.
    Fortune. Medium green. Quick growing. May be started under glass in February.
    Suzan. Pale green. Also for starting under glass in February.
    Tom Thumb. Very early. Very small and compact: useful for catch-cropping.

Crispheads:
    Avoncrisp. Of Great Lakes type (see below) but more compact.
    Great Lakes. Large solid head. Withstands hot weather.
    Webbs Wonderful. Very large head. Very crisp.
    Windermere. Of Great Lakes type but smaller and more compact. Recommended for October cold frame sowing.

Looseheads:
    Grand Rapids. Good for both summer growing outdoors and greenhouse culture in winter.
    Salad Bowl. Mature plant resembles curled endive in appearance. Crisp. Withstands hot, dry weather.

For over-wintering outdoors:
    Valdor. Large, solid heads of cabbage type.
    Winter Density. See above.

For sowing in frames and cloches:
    May King. Large heads.
    Unrivalled. Medium size heads.

For greenhouse culture:
    Kloek. For sowing in October, cutting in March.
    Knap. For sowing in October, cutting in April.
    Kwiek. For sowing in August, cutting in midwinter.
    Premier. Recommended for starting in heat and later transplanting outdoors.

CORN SALAD
    Large Leaved.

CELERY
    Giant Pink. Very pale colour.
    Giant Red. Deep colour.
    Giant White. Large, solid sticks.

Self-blanching:
    Golden Self-blanching. Compact and quick-maturing.

Green:
    American Green. Pale green. Does not require earthing.

CHICORY
  Witloof or Brussels.
  Sugar Loaf (Pain de Sucre).

ENDIVE
  Green Curled.
  Batavian Broad Leaved.

RADISH
  Cherry Belle. Very early and crisp.
    Mild flavour.
  French Breakfast. Cylindrical roots,
    scarlet with white tips. Mild
    flavour.
  Inca. Globe-shaped. Bright scarlet.
    Roots remain crisp over long
    period.
  Long White Icicle. Long white roots.
  Scarlet Globe. Bright red.
  Sparkler. Globe-shaped. Bright scarlet,
    white-tipped.

WINTER RADISH
  Black Spanish. Black skin. White flesh.
    Turnip-shaped
  China Rose. Rose-coloured skin. White
    flesh. Long, blunt-ended roots.

long-term crops

A small portion of the vegetable garden should be set aside for the perennial crops which will come up year after year. Some of these — globe artichokes for example — do not last long but others are really long term and it is worth going to considerable trouble to prepare the ground thoroughly in advance of planting. A well made asparagus bed can continue to be productive for 30 years.

1   Asparagus can be started from seed. Sow in April, rows 30 cm (12 in) apart and thin to 23 cm (9 in). Transplant to the permanent bed the next April.

2   Start preparing the asparagus bed in autumn, digging thoroughly to improve drainage and eradicate all perennial weeds.

3   In early winter dig in rotted farmyard or stable manure or garden compost liberally and fork the surface over in February.

4   Most people start by buying roots. Buy good one-year-old plants: nothing is gained from securing older crowns which are more difficult to re-establish.

5   In April take out trenches 90 cm (3 ft) apart, 30 cm (12 in) wide and 20 cm (8 in) deep with a slight mound in the middle.

6   Immediately the crowns arrive plant 23 cm (9 in) apart, spreading the roots out in the trench.

7   Return soil to the trench until the roots are covered by only 7.5 cm (3 in).

8   During the summer, as you hoe to keep down annual weeds, let soil gradually fill the trench.

23 cm. (9 in.) deep.

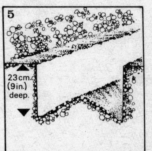

9 Late every February feed the asparagus bed with a dressing of general garden fertiliser, 105 g per sq m (3 oz per sq yd).

10 Cut no shoots the year of planting and only the odd sample stem the next year. The second year after planting stop cutting after 5 weeks, subsequently after 6 weeks.

11 Cut the stems about 7.5 cm (3 in) below the surface. Use of a proper serrated asparagus knife makes this easier.

12 Let the fern grow in summer, supporting it with strings. Pick off all berries to prevent a crop of seedlings over the bed.

13 Sow globe artichoke seed in shallow drills 30 cm (12 in) apart in April. Thin to 15 cm (6 in) and move to permanent bed a year after sowing.

14 Alternatively, prepare a bed of rich soil, buy young plants in April and plant firmly 60 cm (24 in) apart, rows 76 cm (30 in) apart.

15 Cut artichoke flower heads for eating before any colour shows. A bed should crop well for three years.

16 Remove dead foliage in autumn. In April sever rooted offsets from their parent plants to make a new bed.

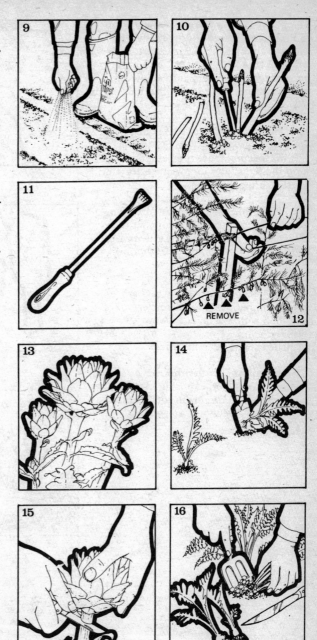

17 Plant mint in March, laying 7.5 cm (3 in) lengths of root horizontally over the bed, about 13 cm (5 in) apart. Cover with 3.5 cm (1½ in) of the fine soil. To prevent roots spreading into adjoining ground surround the bed with a barrier of buried slates, old tiles or bricks.

18 Plant horseradish roots in March in deeply dug ground, 30 cm (12 in) apart. Lift in November, use the best roots and keep the remainder in not-quite-dry sand for replanting in March.

19 Plant rhubarb crowns in March in deeply dug, well manured soil. Set them 90 cm (3 ft) apart, with the growth tips of the crown just exposed. Gather no stems the first year.

20 In January cover a few rhubarb roots with old barrels, buckets or boxes and then with a blanket of strawy manure, compost or leaves. This will give blanched stems early in spring.

21 Obtain still earlier rhubarb by lifting roots in November, exposing to frost for a few days, and forcing in total darkness beneath the greenhouse staging.

long-term crops — recommended varieties

ASPARAGUS
From seed:
    Connover's Colossal
    Martha Washington

From plants:
    Regal Pedigree
    KBF (Kidner's Pedigree)
    Connover's Colossal

GLOBE ARTICHOKE
From seed:
    Green Globe
    Green Ball

From plants:
    Gros Vert de Laon

MINT
    Apple or Round-leaved mint (*Mentha rotundifolia*, Bowles' variety), much better than the common Spearmint (*Mentha spicata*).

HORSERADISH
    No varieties

RHUBARB
    Early: Timperley Early
    Second-early: Hawke's Champagne
    Maincrop: The Sutton

miscellaneous vegetables — recommended varieties

AUBERGINE (Egg Plant)
    Long Purple

CAPSICUM (Sweet Pepper)
    Ace, Canape, Worldbeater

MARROWS
Trailing types:
    Table Dainty, Long White, Long Green, Little Gem
Bush types:
    Early Gem, Long White Bush, Long Green Bush, Zucchini.
Courgette types:
    Green Bush Fl hybrid, Zucchini Fl hybrid,
    Golden Zucchini
Squash types:
    Butternut, Vegetable Spaghetti
Pumpkins:
    Hundredweight

SEAKALE
    Lily White

SWEET CORN
    Earliking, Early Xtra Sweet, First of All, Kelvedon Glory, North Star

miscellaneous vegetables

There are a few vegetables which do not fit into the usual groups, the leaf or green crops, the roots, the pod-bearers, round which our vegetable plot rotation is planned. Some of these "loners", for instance marrows, are among the most widely grown of all vegetables and some, seakale for example, are uncommon, real connoisseur's vegetables, yet all are worthy of your consideration. Here we deal with aubergines, capsicums, the marrow family, seakale and sweet corn.

1   The aubergine or egg plant must have warmth. Sow in a heated greenhouse (18° C, 65° F) in January, prick out the seedlings separately into small pots and later move into 15 cm (6 in) pots.

2   The aubergines may either be fruited in the greenhouse or, in late May, hardened off and planted outdoors beneath cloches, 60 cm (2 ft) apart in the row.

3   Capsicums or sweet peppers are grown in the same way as aubergines but will tolerate a little less warmth.

4   In very favoured districts, after starting under glass, capsicums will ripen in the open. Never eat the seeds: cut these out before cooking.

5   Vegetable marrows, squashes, pumpkins and courgettes all belong to the same family and are grown in the same way. None of them will stand any frost.

6   About mid-April sow seeds in pairs, on edge, in small pots. Cover with glass and newspaper until germination.

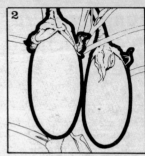

150

7   When the seedlings are growing sturdily, pinch out the weaker of each pair. Protect from frost until early June and then plant outdoors.

8   Meanwhile, prepare the marrow bed. Contrary to popular ideas, a heap is unnecessary and plants grown on heaps need very frequent watering.

9   Marrows do, however, like very rich, moisture-holding soil. For each trailing plant take out a hole 60 cm (2 ft) across and 30 cm (1 ft) deep. For bush marrows take out a 30 cm (1 ft) deep trench.

10   Work manure generously into the bottom of hole or trench. Replace the top soil but leave a ridge round the edge of the hole or along the sides of the trench. This will facilitate later watering.

11   Plant trailing marrows 1.2 m (4 ft) apart, pumpkins and bush marrows 90 cm (3 ft). Protect from slugs with slug pellets.

12   Where no glass protection is available, sow seeds outdoors in situ at the end of May.

13   To ensure good pollination in indifferent weather thrust the centres of male flowers into the centres of female.

14   To prevent damage by slugs and contact with moist soil, lift marrows and pumpkins on to sheets of glass, slates or old tiles.

15   Courgettes are simply very prolific varieties of bush marrow. Cut when about 10 cm (4 in) long. Left to grow, they make large marrows but further production ceases.

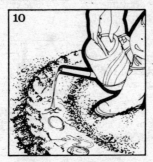

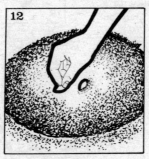

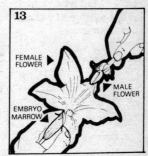

FEMALE FLOWER

MALE FLOWER

EMBRYO MARROW

16   For seakale, buy root cuttings in March and plant in rich soil 30 cm (12 in) apart, rows 45 cm (18 in) apart.

17   From November on lift roots and force in darkness as for rhubarb (p. 147, frame 21) or blanch in situ with a large inverted pot.

18   Start sweet corn in small pots under glass in April, sowing two seeds per pot, later reducing to the stronger seedling. Plant outdoors when frost risk has passed, without disturbing the roots.

19   Alternatively, sow sweet corn in situ in early May. Plant, or sow, 45 cm (18 in) apart each way in blocks of at least four rows to aid pollination.

20   Cut sweet corn cobs when the silk tassel at the top has withered brown . . .

21   . . . and when a little milky juice exudes when you puncture a grain with your thumbnail.

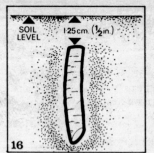

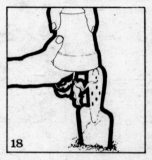

miscellaneous vegetable operations

exhibiting vegetables

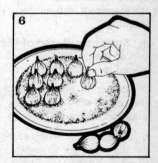

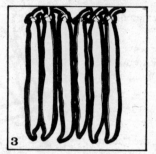

The general points made on page 84 apply just as appropriately to vegetables as to fruit. Show vegetables should be quite clean, fresh and free from blemish. Unless a class is specifically for giant specimens, size should be what is suitable for table use and quality is paramount. All the vegetables on one dish should be of the same variety and of equal size.

1   Take great care in harvesting, transporting and staging exhibition vegetables not to spoil their natural bloom, particularly in handling pea pods.

2   Potatoes and other root vegetables should be gently washed clean, never scrubbed. Keep moist and in the dark until the show.

3   With French and runner beans, straightness of pod and evenness of size are important. Stalks should be intact.

4   Cabbages are best if it has not been necessary to remove defective outer leaves. Trim the outer leaves of cauliflowers to within 5 cm (2 in) of the curd.

5   Stand onions on cardboard rings or shaped wads of paper. Bulbs should be firm with thin necks, the stems neatly turned over and tied.

6   Shallot bulbs will stand neatly "to attention" on a bed of dry sand.

7   For a collection choose from the vegetables which are more difficult to grow well and therefore stand to gain more points — asparagus, carrots, cauliflowers, celery, leeks, mushrooms, onions, peas, potatoes, seakale, tomatoes.

storing vegetables

Although root vegetables will often be safe from anything but exceptionally hard frost if left where they have grown, they always remain fair game for slugs and other soil pests. It is not only safer to lift and store carefully but it also frees the ground for digging. A supply for immediate use should always be kept indoors to be available when hard frost makes lifting and clamp-opening difficult or impossible.

1   BEETROOTS. Twist the leaves off before storing. This seals the stem fibres and prevents the quality-spoiling bleeding which follows cutting.

2   The point of twisting must be a hand's breadth away from the root.

3   Tap roots at the base of the beet may be trimmed back to 2.5 cm (1 in) from the main root without risk of serious bleeding.

4   Store a small crop of beetroots in a box of moderately dry sand or peat placed in a frost-free place.

5   Larger quantities of roots may be stacked on sand or peat on the floor of a shed and covered with more sand or peat.

6   CARROTS. Before storing these roots cut the leaves off as close to the crown as possible.

7   If you cut through the crown, the root will shrivel in store. If you leave too long stems, they will grow and the roots spoil.

8   Store carrots in the same way as beetroots or put in an outdoor clamp. For this dig a circular trench, throwing excavated soil to the centre.

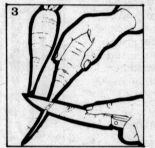

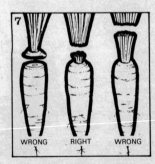

WRONG   RIGHT   WRONG

9   Tread this round platform firm and lay down a ring of carrots pointing to the centre, radius 60 cm (2 ft) less than that of the trench circle.

10   Fill in with more rings until the first layer is complete.

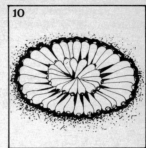

11   Start a second layer with a ring slightly smaller than the first.

12   Continue with this pile, tapering to its apex.

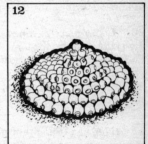

13   Thatch roughly, about 30 cm (1 ft) deep, with straw or bracken, placed with stems upright.

14   Now deepen and extend the circular trench round the heap, throwing soil over the straw.

15   Start from the bottom and cover the straw upwards in stages, compacting the soil with the back of the spade as you work.

16   POTATOES. These too may be stored in a circular clamp, like carrots, but for larger crops a long-shaped clamp is necessary, dimensions as here.

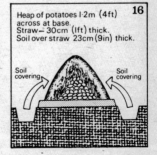

Heap of potatoes 1·2m (4ft) across at base.
Straw– 30cm (1ft) thick.
Soil over straw 23cm (9in) thick.

Soil covering

Soil covering

17 Spread the potatoes on the soil surface, in dry weather, for several hours before clamping but be ready to cover in the event of rain.

18 Leave the clamp open for several days, but protected from any rain, to allow sweating before finally covering the clamp in.

19 ONIONS. These are best roped. After sun-drying cut the dead leaves back to about 10 cm (4 in).

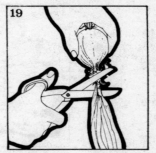

20 Take a piece of rope about 1 m (or 1 yd) long and tie the largest onion to one end, using wisps of raffia or string.

21 Continue up to the top and make a loop in the rope.

22 Hang in a frost-proof place. Dry, airy and cool conditions are essential.

23 VEGETABLE MARROWS. If really dry and ripe, these may be stored until Christmas under straw in an outhouse.

24 But a safer way is to hang each marrow individually in a sling of netting and suspend in a cool, airy, frost-proof place.

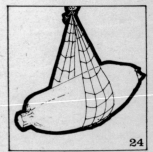

vegetable trouble shooting

Generally speaking, garden vegetables are remarkably free from pest and disease troubles. Nevertheless a few must be expected. If guarded against much disappointment will be avoided. In some gardens birds can be a great nuisance. In such cases some of the precautions described on p. 74 may be adapted. Most other pests will have to be dealt with by spraying and the precautions outlined on pp. 75 and 76 should be observed.

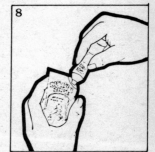

1 *Aphids* (greenfly and blackfly) of various kinds attack many crops. Curling leaves are often the first sign noticed. Spraying with a systemic insecticide will reach even pests protected by curled leaves.

2 *Blackfly* almost inevitably invade broad beans and often runners. Forestall by spraying (see p. 116, frames 13 and 14) but if crops are soon to be eaten use a safe, non-poisonous insecticide.

3 *Cabbage root fly* is often the cause of plants of the cabbage family (including turnips and radishes) wilting in summer.

4 If you dig up collapsed plants, you may find the culprit at the roots, the maggot of the cabbage root fly.

5 Burn attacked plants with soil adhering. Spray round each plant with gamma-BHC within 4 days of planting. See also p.98, frame 8.

6 *Carrot fly maggots* burrow into the roots, occasionally also attacking parsnips and celery. Early June or later sowings may escape.

7 After thinning carrots always firm the soil by treading and then watering. Never leave thinnings lying on the ground.

8 To prevent carrot fly attack, before sowing dust the seed with gamma-BHC seed dressing.

9   Or sprinkle gamma-BHC dust along the open drills when sowing carrots.

10 *Cats* may dig up newly-sown seed-beds. Sprinkle the bed with garden pepper dust.

11 *Caterpillars* of the cabbage white butterfly (A) and of the cabbage moth (B) devour the leaves. Hand pick the caterpillars and spray with derris or dust with derris powder.

12 *Chafer beetle grubs* eating the roots cause plants to collapse suddenly. Any may be attacked but lettuce are favourites. Burn affected plants, search soil for grubs and dust ground with gamma-BHC powder.

13 *Club root disease* may attack any member of the cabbage family, distorting roots, stunting growth and killing. Dress infected soil with hydrated lime before planting 280 g per sq m (½ lb per sq yd) and dip roots in calomel paste (see p. 98 frame 8).

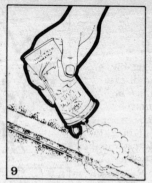

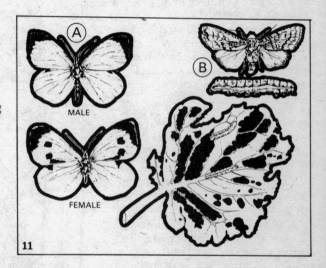

14 *Cutworms* chew plant stems at ground level by night. Hand pick and dust soil with gamma-BHC dust.

15 *Flea beetles* may eat holes in cabbage, turnip and radish leaves in dry weather. Spray with gamma-BHC.

16 *Leaf-miners* burrow in celery leaves, causing blisters which can be pinched. Spray larger infestations with malathion.

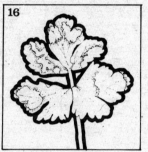

17 *Mice* may eat seedlings to ground level. Set traps, poison with warfarin and see p. 121, frames 47 and 48.

18 *Millipedes,* slow-moving insects, feed on plant roots. Work gamma-BHC dust into top soil before sowing or planting, but don't plant potatoes (see p. 103, frame 4). Don't confuse with —

19 *Centipedes,* fast-moving helpful creatures with one pair of legs per body segment. Millipedes have two pairs of legs per segment, curl when disturbed.

20 *Pea and bean weevils* scallop leaf edges and can seriously damage young plants. Dust with gamma-BHC powder.

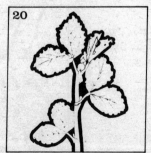

21 *Pea thrips,* or thunder flies, attack leaves and pods. Spray with fenitrothion as first flowers open and repeat in 14 days.

22 *Pea moths* lay in June and July. The grubs enter the pods and feed on the peas. Control: as for pea thrips, see frame 21.

23 *Potato blight disease* first reveals itself, after midsummer, as dark spots on leaves, possibly with delicate white fungus on the underside.

24 In a few weeks the disease can spread through the plants, killing foliage and infecting tubers causing them to rot. There is no cure for potato blight.

25 To prevent potato blight, from late June (in south-west) to mid-July (in north-east and Scotland), spray with copper, maneb or zineb fungicide. Repeat twice at fortnightly intervals.

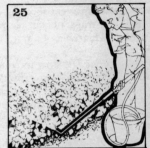

26 *Common scab,* disfiguring the skin of potatoes, occurs in soils lacking humus. Avoid lime and line the planting drill with peat.

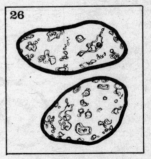

27 *Slugs* always seem to be with us, eating potatoes (above), bush tomatoes, marrows, cucumbers lying on the soil, eating into cabbages and lettuces, killing seedlings. Scatter slug pellets according to maker's directions.

28 *Turnip gall weevil* is easily confused with club root but the grub responsible may be found in cut-open roots. Control as for cabbage root fly.

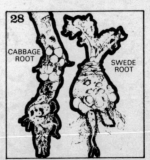

CABBAGE ROOT

SWEDE ROOT

29 *Wireworms* attack the roots of most crops. Dust the soil with gamma-BHC powder but see p. 103, frame 4.